HAPPY FAMILIES?

John Drane *is a writer and theologian, and a gifted popular communicator. His previous books,* Evangelism for a New Age *and* What is the New Age Saying to the Church? *are both published by Marshall Pickering, an imprint of HarperCollinsPublishers.*

For ten years Olive Drane *has been a chairperson of Children's Hearings (part of the Scottish legal system which deals with offences committed by and against children). She is also noted for her involvement with the arts in worship and evangelism.*

John and Olive *teach regularly together at Fuller Seminary, Pasadena and have also lectured at Regent College, Vancouver as well as being key speakers at Spring Harvest and similar events. Their Christian ministry ranges from running children's groups and facilitating parenting groups to leading workshops on creative spirituality to enable adults to come to terms with the scars their childhood experiences have left.* John and Olive *have been married for over 25 years and have three living children.*

HANDBOOKS OF PASTORAL CARE
SERIES EDITOR: MARLENE COHEN

HAPPY FAMILIES?

JOHN DRANE &
OLIVE M. FLEMING DRANE

Marshall Pickering
An Imprint of HarperCollins*Publishers*

HarperCollins*Publishers*
77–85 Fulham Palace Road, London W6 8JB

First published in Great Britain
in 1995 by HarperCollins*Publishers*

1 3 5 7 9 10 8 6 4 2

A catalogue record for this book is
available from the British Library

ISBN 0 551 02854–8

Typeset by Harper Phototypesetters Limited
Northampton, England
Printed and bound in Great Britain by
HarperCollinsManufacturing Glasgow

CONTENTS

SERIES INTRODUCTION

The demand for pastoral care and counselling in churches has increased to record levels and every indication is that this trend will continue to accelerate. Some churches are fortunate to have ready access to professionally trained and qualified counsellors, but in most situations this onerous task falls to pastors.

Some pastors* are naturally gifted for the ministry of counselling. Some receive training before ordination and then seek to extend this as opportunity permits through the years. Others have the task of counselling thrust upon them. Most seem to feel some sustained demand, internal or external, to be competent in the field. This series aims to address some of the gaps frequently left in theological training. It is intended to offer support to those entrusted with responsibility for the care and well-being of others.

Comparative studies of healing agencies were pioneered in the United States. As long as thirty years ago The Joint Commission on Mental Illness reported that 42 per cent of 2,460 people canvassed would go first to the clergy with any mental health problem.

Of course there may be reasons other than overtly religious for a preference for clergy counselling. There may seem less stigma in seeing a pastor than a psychiatrist. Also, viewing a problem as a primarily spiritual matter may preclude taking some degree of

*The term 'pastor' is used generically here, to include all who have a recognized pastoral role within a local church or Christian community.

responsibility for it and for examining its depths. And, of course, clergy visits are cheaper! Unfortunately, there can be the additional reason that parishoners feel an inappropriate right of access to their pastor's time and skills. God's availability at all times is sometimes confused with ours, as is divine omniscience.

Being a front-line mental health worker can put a pastor under enormous and inappropriate strain. Counselling is becoming the primary time consumer in an increasing number of parish ministries.

Feeling unsafe and inadequate in any situation inevitably produces some form of self-protective behaviour, unless we can admit our inadequacy while retaining self-respect. Religious professionals who are under pressure to function as counsellors but know their skills and knowledge to be in other areas may understandably take refuge in various defences, even dogmatism. The term 'religious professional' is more familiar in some countries than in others. The clerical profession actually preceded all others, in status and in time. 'But what are we professional at?' can be a difficult question to answer. This is especially so when clergy are driven to believe that anything short of multi-competence will let God down.

Pastors may feel obliged not to appear inadequate in the area of counselling because of their confidence that the Bible contains the answer to every human need. And it does, conceptually. The difficulty is not with the Bible nor with the pastor's knowledge of the Bible. Neither of these should be in question. The concern is whether pastors have the additional ability of a clinician. Naming a counselling problem correctly – not the presenting problem but the real, underlying issues and their components – is a refined specialism. Making a faulty diagnosis, especially when God and biblical authority are somehow implicated, is the cause of much damage. Clinical terminology can be applied almost at random but with a surprising degree of assurance. Understanding the Bible, and understanding the complexities of clinical practice, are not one and the same skill. In 1985 a comparative study was conducted into the ability of 112 clergy to recognize 13 signs of suicidal tendencies. (Reported in the *Journal of Psychology and Theology*: 1989: Vol 17: No 2.) It was found that clergy were unable to recognize these signs any better than educated lay people and substantially less well than other mental health workers. This is no necessary reflection on the clergy. Why should they be expected to have this professional ability? Considering them culpable would only be just if they were to assume, or to allow an assumption to go unchecked, that their skills were identical to those of other caring professionals.

One pressure is that graduates of some theological colleges have actually been taught that ordination will confer counselling skills. 'We must insist upon the idea that every man who has been called of God into the ministry has been given the basic gifts for . . . counselling' (Jay Adams, *The Christian Counsellor's Manual*, 1973, Presbyterian and Reformed Publishing Company; Part One, Page 20).

Equating a ministry calling with being a gifted counsellor could be seen to involve some leaping assumptions. These are becoming more apparent as we distinguish what we used to call 'the ministry' from God's calling of *all* believers into ministry. As more work is done on what we mean by 'ordination' more clergy can be released into those areas of ministry for which they are clearly gifted and suited.

Belief that counselling skills are divinely bestowed in conjunction with a ministry 'call' will probably not issue in the purchase of this series of handbooks! Other pastors who believe or fear that neither counselling nor any other skills can be taken for granted, are possibly conducting their ministries under some heavy burdens. This series is written with a concern to address these burdens and to redress some erroneous equations that relate to them. Each author has extensive experience in some avenue of ministry and is also trained and experienced in some aspect of counselling.

These Handbooks of Pastoral Care are designed to aid pastors in assessing the needs of those who come to them for help. The more accurately this assessment can be made the more confident the pastor can be about the form of ministry that is required in each instance. Sometimes pastors will decide to refer the matter elsewhere, but on other occasions there can be a prayerful assurance in retaining the counselling role within their own ministry.

Marlene Cohen
Oxford, March 1994

PREFACE

Writing this book has been quite a challenge. For one thing, sociologists, psychologists, lawyers, and counselling agencies of all kinds have conducted an enormous amount of research on the family in recent years, and it has not been easy to take account of all that in a way that would be helpful in the essentially practical context of a Christian series entitled *Handbooks of Pastoral Care*. Moreover, the series itself contains other volumes that, in one way and another, impinge on our topic, including books on sexuality, on marriage, and on loss. In trying to be as comprehensive as possible without trespassing into areas which more properly belong elsewhere in the series, we have aimed to focus on those aspects of the subject which are distinctively concerned with the ways people live together in the community of the home.

The book falls into two main sections. First of all, it gives an overview of the state of the family in contemporary Western culture, tracing the historical and social pathway that has led us to where we are today. We identify some of the major aspects of family life as it affects the lives of children, women, and men. It is important for Christians to appreciate this larger context, as it provides many useful clues for understanding how we might most effectively support the modern family. All families – including those which may seem to have no real 'problems' – are wrestling with the issues highlighted in this section of the book, and most of the practical questions that arise in ministering to the family are variations on this one collection of common themes.

As Christians, our thinking should also be rooted within the biblical tradition and include the teaching of the Church. Christians can have unrealistic expectations of family life, fuelled by an inaccurate perception of what Bible families were actually like, and combined with a culturally-conditioned use of carefully selected Bible passages. Many Christian adults carry an enormous burden of guilt because their actual families do not match their imagined image of the 'ideal Christian family'. In the effort to avoid that, we have deliberately come to the Bible only after our examination of the modern Western family. That way we can read the Bible in the light of the actual questions with which people wrestle, rather than constructing an abstract and theoretical analysis of Bible teaching which is remote and distant from the average person's experience.

After that, we move on to ask how the Church can help families in a rapidly-changing world. There are no easy quick-fix solutions, but there are many things that will helpfully channel God's love into the homes associated with our congregations, as well as more widely into the community. After a brief look at the need to make churches more family-friendly, we mention some specific areas in which churches can work in positive ways to enhance family life, before commenting in the final chapter on pastoral issues relating to family crisis. If the major focus of our attention there is on domestic violence and abuse, then that reflects growing awareness of this major threat to family relationships, as well as the fact that other aspects of relational breakdown are covered in more depth by other books in this series.

We need to make two acknowledgements and a disclaimer. First the acknowledgements. In the initial stages of research for this book we were fortunate to have the assistance of Larissa Clark, who was at that time a graduate student at Golden Gate Baptist Theological Seminary in San Francisco. Over an extended period during 1993, she interviewed clergy and other church leaders in both Britain and the USA. The results of her survey provided a significant insight into how churches of different traditions are ministering to families, and the kind of advice that is typically given to families when they seek help in times of difficulty. Over the same period, we have also enjoyed getting to know series editor Marlene Cohen, and her personal openness in discussing some of the issues raised here has been a major encouragement to us.

Now the disclaimer. As a result of many opportunities to minister together among Christians in different parts of the world, we are well aware of the ways Western people tend to impose their values and lifestyles on other cultures. We have learned much from Christians of other nations, not least about families. We know that the Western experience of family is not the only possible one, nor do we believe that it is necessarily the most truly Christian one. To have written this book on a cross-cultural basis would have been exciting for us – and may be something that needs to be done in the future. But at this point in time we had to draw the line somewhere, and limitations of time and space mean that this is essentially a book about the status of the Western family, and the opportunities for Christian ministry within that context. On occasion we have made brief reference to other possible family structures, but we have been unable to say as much about them as we sometimes would have liked.

We have each brought to this book different skills and experience. For ten years, Olive has been a chairperson of Children's Hearings (part of the Scottish legal system that deals with offences committed by and against children). We have also worked together in Christian ministry in activities as diverse as running groups for children, facilitating parenting groups in church, and leading workshops on creative spirituality to help adults come to terms with the scars left by their own traumatic childhood experiences. We have drawn on all these things here, as well as reflecting on our shared experience of trying to create a family home that would reflect the values of God's kingdom by providing a safe and secure environment for those who live in it.

The topics covered here could be addressed in different ways, and many of them continue to be the subject of heated debates among Christians, based on issues of theology and morality. At an early stage we decided not to engage with these debates, but rather to concentrate on practical pastoral issues. People suffer hurt and breakdown for various reasons, and we are called to minister to people in need, regardless of what we might think about the rights and wrongs of certain kinds of behaviour. Our own conclusions have been born out of the struggle actually to be Christian in today's changing world, and inasmuch as we present a theological understanding of the family, then that arises out of reflection on our experience in the light of Christian history and the Bible. For us, this journey of exploration is not yet over, and if what we have written encourages others to join us on the road, it will have fulfilled our hopes.

John & Olive Drane
Mothering Sunday 1995

A FAMILY PRAYER

Creator God,

You have placed each one of us in a family.

One day it seems like a stroke of genius on your part;
Another day it can feel as if you made a big mistake.

In our family relationships we experience the height of
acceptance, and the depth of rejection:
    — the excitement of finding you, even as we discover
    our true selves through sharing with those we love;
    — the spiritual claustrophobia of evil forces, as we
    injure and damage those who are closest to us.

You are the one from whom all families seek blessing.

You are our caring Father, our loving Mother, our
protective Brother and our ever-watchful Sister.

We are women, men, and children created in your glorious
image. Bring us through the pain of repentance into the
freedom of your forgiveness. Make us whole, that we may
bring healing to our families.

Come, Holy Spirit, renew and restore our homes.

We pray in Jesus' name

Amen.

FAMILY HISTORY

Images of the Ideal Family

The cheerfu' supper done, wi' serious face
They, round the ingle, form a circle wide;
The sire turns o'er, wi' patriarchal grace,
The big ha'-Bible, ance his father's pride.
...
He wales a portion with judicious care,
And 'Let us worship God!' he says, with solemn air.

The words come from the pen of the celebrated eighteenth-century Scottish poet Robert Burns, but the time and place could be anywhere in the Western world during the last 200 years or so. In so far as there is a widely-held concept of the ideal family, then the imagery of Burns's poem *The Cotter's Saturday Night* has captured its spirit exactly. It may not correspond to the reality of how families today live, but nevertheless it is still the model to which many aspire, especially Christians.

The poem begins with a graphic description of the simple working man returning to his cottage after a hard week's work, to be welcomed by his eager children and greeted by the smile of his wife who has made their rough home as warm and comforting as she possibly can for his arrival. This family enjoys warm and generous, if predictable, relationships. Children and parents gather round the fire for a cosy Saturday night spent in one another's company, in a place of safety and security dutifully preserved by the mother as a shelter from the harsher world outside, in which not only the father but also their elder daughter has worked during the preceding week. Burns deftly paints a vivid word picture of the father's physical and emotional renewal in the company of those whom he loves and provides for, while the mother (who features explicitly only briefly) takes pride in the fact that her working daughter has brought home a young man with whom she is clearly in love, and thereby the succession of this lifestyle is ensured for the next generation. But the centrepiece of the poem is the way the family finds its identity and sense of purpose by being focused around moral and religious values: the father reads the Bible, and leads his family in worship of God. Indeed, a later line in the poem describes him as 'The saint, the father, and the husband . . .': he may be powerless in terms of the way prosperity is understood by the harsh world outside the family home, but in the home he and his family enjoy spiritual qualities of such magnitude that 'The cottage leaves the palace far behind . . .'.

This is not a distinctively Scottish understanding of family life. The same image can be found just as easily and, if anything, even more extensively presented, in the work of the nineteenth-century English novelist Charles Dickens. In *A Christmas Carol*, one of Dickens's best-known works, the one sight which eventually moves the miserable Scrooge to change his attitudes to those less well off than himself is when he is taken in a dream to look through the window of the home of his employee Bob Cratchit. There, a man previously known to Scrooge only as a cog in the economic machinery of the workplace suddenly takes on a wholly different identity. Just like the cotter of Burns's poem, the unfortunate Cratchit comes alive in the company of his family, and reveals a more profoundly human side to his life and personality than the one that normally engages with the world of everyday work. After a hard day's labour in an office from which all vestiges of humanitarian spirit have, as a matter of policy, been systematically eliminated, the warm fireside and the open generosity of wife and children are just what Cratchit needs to recharge his batteries before returning once more to the drudgery which is Scrooge's daily business. He may be poor, but he is a good provider within his means. Cratchit gives his family financial security, while his wife supplies comfort and affirmation, and the children live in happy dependence on their parents, in blissful ignorance of the harsh realities with which their father wrestles day by day – their innocent vulnerability highlighted through the character of Tiny Tim, the handicapped child whose plight eventually melts even Scrooge's hard heart.

The same sentimental images can as easily be found in North American culture. Think, for example, of the writings of Laura Ingalls Wilder, whose vivid images of family life in the pioneering days (based on her own childhood experience) have been taken to every corner of the world through the popular and long-running TV series *Little House on the Prairie*. One of the reasons this series has continued to be so popular over a period of more than forty years is undoubtedly because it depicts a family lifestyle that, though bearing little resemblance to the way most families actually live today, still evokes a strong sense of admiration for the values of people who managed to hold their families together in the face of considerable economic and social hardship, coupled with a nostalgic feeling that, if only we could somehow manage to get back to that way of life, things would be much easier in the modern world.[1]

Christians and the Family

In family life, as in everything else, it is impossible to turn the clock back. Nevertheless, this kind of romantic idealism is still deeply embedded in the thinking of many people, Christians in particular. Moreover, some Christians have exalted the alleged virtues of this style of being family to the point where it has been given almost a sacred status, as 'the Christian family'. When people call from time to time for a return to 'family values', these are invariably the values they have in mind. Yet the perpetuation of this image as being the 'Christian' family raises at least as many questions as it purports to solve. For one thing, it does not match reality for a majority of people. Virtually no-one can live this way in today's world, Christians included, and the only groups who come anywhere near it are communities such as the Amish, who have taken a conscious decision to distance themselves from everything that characterizes modern life. The truth is that for most others, the suggestion that family life could or should be like this is bad news. Some Christians might make the effort to recreate the images and social structures of yesteryear, but in striving to do so most only succeed in adding to the burden of guilt that already oppresses the lives of so many within the Church. At the same time, people outside the Church are likely to dismiss this lifestyle as irrelevant to the options available to them, and along with what is perceived as an outmoded Christian response to changing social realities, they might easily dismiss everything else related to the Gospel.

These pragmatic questions are by no means secondary. But the perpetuation of this one model of family as being the only authentically Christian model raises other urgent questions. In particular, we must ask whether there is in fact such a thing as a specifically 'Christian family'. If we take the Bible as the starting point for Christian beliefs and values, then it certainly provides no blueprint for any such social entity. Indeed, as we shall see in a later chapter, there is not one single Bible family that corresponds to this modern image. The fact of the matter is that the notion of family means different things to different people and different cultures – and always has. Though it might be true to say that 'the family' provides one of the significant building blocks of society, those blocks have never all been the same shape as one another, and throughout history Christians have followed the norms and conventions of the cultures in which they lived by accepting, supporting and perpetuating many different models of family. Our starting point here is the conviction that it is misleading and unhelpful to talk of the 'Christian family'. In reality, there is no such thing. It is more accurate to say that there are families, some of which are Christian. The challenges and difficulties faced in the home by Christians are exactly the same as those with which other people struggle. This is why the creation of family-friendly churches can play a significant part not only in the internal workings of the Christian community, but also in the fulfilment of its missionary calling to share the good news with others who are as yet not Christian.

Family in Context

What then is a family? Over recent decades, a major research industry has grown up around that question. Scholars of many disciplines have addressed this issue from the perspective of their own insights. They include sociologists, anthropologists, economists, psychoanalysts, politicians, historians, and lawyers, as well as leaders within different faith communities.[2] This book is not intended to be a philosophical treatise on the nature of the family. Our primary focus is on practical theology, and though we have drawn extensively on the researches of many other people, it is not our intention to review their findings here except in so far as they impinge on the Church's pastoral role. Indeed, so much has been written and said on the topic that in the context of a small book there is no way we can adequately explore all the nuances of the question, let alone review all the possible answers to it. It is however important that we set our contemporary understanding of 'the family', and of the Church's opportunities and responsibilities in ministering to and equipping 'the family', within a wider perspective that will enable us to identify as clearly as possible the nature of the issues with which we have to deal. Within this frame of reference, perhaps the most useful entry point into understanding the contemporary debate about 'the family' will be to take a quick backward glance at our own history, and trace the origins of some current assumptions and expectations. A proper historical perspective can give profound insights into our present situation. Henry Ford got it wrong when he said in 1916 that 'History is more or less bunk . . . we want to live in the present and the only history that is worth a tinker's damn is the history we make today.'[3] The exact opposite is in fact true, and the choices we have available today arise directly out of our past. An old Chinese proverb encapsulates it well: 'Those who do not know the village they have

come from will never find the village they are looking for.' In order
to see who we might yet become we need to own who we are, and
to be aware of some of the factors that have made us this way.
Nowhere is this more strikingly true than in the family.

People are made to live in community, and relationships between
people are a fundamental part of being human. But from the very
dawn of time, the set of relationships that characterize families have
always been regarded as distinctive and special. In relational terms,
there are two unique characteristics that identify a set of relationships as occurring within a family, namely the significance of the
gender roles occupied by male and female, and the corresponding
differentiation between parents and children. The practical outcomes
of the power dynamic implied in these two sets of relationships
might vary in different circumstances. But they constitute the fundamental defining elements of those forms of relationship that have
always been identified as family. All other distinctive aspects of
family life arise out of or are related to these two main areas. In her
1993 study, *The Family in Question*, Diana Gittins lists four fundamental characteristics of the family: common residence, economic
co-operation, reproduction, and sexuality. These characteristics in
turn imply further elements that all generally impinge on the concept of family, including such things as the nature of the power relationships between women and men and adults and children, the
responsibility for domestic labour, parenting roles, sibling relationships, along with understandings of kinship, marriage, and so on held
in the wider community.[4]

Not all families will necessarily display all these characteristics,
especially not today when the whole notion of what constitutes a
family is in a state of so much flux and redefinition, and when several
of these constituent elements are themselves undergoing radical
transformation. With so many substantial notions relevant to the
concept of the family, it is little wonder that there is so much
disagreement as to what the family really is. Nonetheless, this kind
of list provides a useful starting point, and while none of these
elements on their own will point conclusively to a set of relationships that necessarily constitute a family, the criteria proposed by

Gittins serve to give some shape to the debate, and to provide some way of distinguishing family relationships from other forms of human interaction.

What is especially interesting is that once Gittins moves beyond relationships as such, every other characteristic of a family is basically related to economic needs. As far back as it is possible to look historically, the economic purposes of a family have always been primary. The most noteworthy changes in family life have all had their origins in the economic opportunities open to families, and the changes in working patterns that have resulted from that. Contemporary popular images of the family tend to highlight a more romanticized and sentimental concept, in which all the emphasis is on the personal relationships between individual members of a family group, and the notion of what constitutes a family emerges out of that matrix. But the fact is that economic circumstances have always had far more influence in determining the nature of family life than any other single factor. Indeed the nature of work has provided the frame of reference which defined the possible ways in which family members would be able to express and develop their personal relationships. In this respect, today's families are no different from the generations which preceded them.

From Generation to Generation

Like other social institutions, the family remained virtually unchanged for centuries until relatively recent times.[5] Long after the emergence of the great civilizations of the ancient world, the basic pattern for 'the family' differed surprisingly little from the pattern established when our ancestors were hunters and gatherers. In these families economic support, employment, socialization, and education were of fundamental importance, and generally in that order. Families were groups in which people could survive, through which they could find useful things to occupy their time, and within which they could learn how to live with other people. In that context, different family members naturally adopted different roles. In particular, the role of adult men and women tended to be defined by reference to their sexuality (procreation being vital to survival), and to what was practical, which almost amounted to the same thing. The practical considerations that determined appropriate roles were largely determined by the fact that both men and women died at what would nowadays be regarded as a young age, and for women that meant they were either pregnant or suckling children for most of their adult life. Notwithstanding that, the role of women in ancient families was never restricted to what might be called purely domestic work. Or more accurately, domestic work was defined in such a way that it also involved men. In addition, domestic work was productive work in a way that is not generally the case today. In a pre-industrial age, the means of production were essentially based in the home, which meant that everyone who lived there had a significant part to play in the overall economy of the unit. It would be anachronistic to claim that the original ancient family operated on a basis of the recognized equality of all its members, but it is nevertheless true that everyone's role – though different – was of equal importance to the family group. Working together in order to survive was a central feature of all such families.

By and large, this was the pattern of Biblical 'families', where the household unit might typically consist of several generations of different groups of people biologically related to one another, including not only the head of the family and his sexual partner(s) and offspring, but also servants and their relatives, as well as widows, orphans, stateless persons and others who contributed to the economic well-being of the whole, in exchange for which they enjoyed the safety and security of the family unit. Over time – and we can trace this transition in the Bible itself – the nature of family relationships gradually changed, largely under the influence of economic pressures. Once family units were able to build up economic surpluses, the opportunity for trade with other such units also developed. As a consequence, relationships with other household units assumed greater importance than internal family structures, and gradually the base of social organization (which also now began to correlate with state and political organization) became more and more segregated from the household. Because of their greater mobility and physical strength, men tended to be the ones who exercised power in the public sphere outside the family, where matters of property, production, employment and politics became dominant. In due course, such affairs came to be regarded as an exclusively male concern through the development of a patriarchal outlook which confined women to the private sphere of the home, and indeed classified them (and children) as part of the goods with which a man could barter in the wider world of commerce. Women's contribution to the life and economy of the family remained significant and invaluable, but compared with more primitive family structures their role was gradually diminished and squeezed into a much narrower definition of what it meant to be a woman. Of course, none of this happened overnight, and such changes as there were took place almost imperceptibly over many generations, so that there was a natural evolution from ancient times through to the feudal system of the Middle Ages. The driving force behind this change, though, was changing patterns of work. The same thing is still true today, and the developing nature of work is one of the major forces that continues to impact and shape the family unit at the end of the twentieth century.

It is therefore not surprising that between the Middle Ages and today, the most significant transformation in the nature of the family and its values was brought about by changes in the nature of employment, and the economic structure of society. The European Enlightenment, followed by the Industrial Revolution, was the crucible out of which the modern family has been forged. Beginning in the fifteenth century, the first tentative voyages of European explorers led in rapid succession to an expansion of knowledge about astronomy, philosophy, medicine, science and technology so great that, as Western thinkers compared their understanding of things with the previous knowledge of all the great civilizations of the ancient and medieval world, it seemed as if a great light had dawned right across the continent of Europe. The magnitude of the new discoveries made everything that had gone before look like mere superstition, mythology, and intellectual darkness – hence the use of the term 'Enlightenment' to describe this period of modern development. The heritage of the Enlightenment, particularly its rationalist-materialist-reductionist philosophy, continues to have a profound impact on the world today, and it is impossible to understand what is going on in a modern family without taking some account of this. Indeed, almost all the turmoils which we can see in the family today have their origins in this period of Western history.[6]

Industrial Families

Philosophically, one of the key outcomes of this period was the acknowledgement that life could be divided into two spheres. From now on, things would be classified according to whether they belonged in what might be called the public world, concerned with such things as science, economics, politics, and employment, and governed by 'laws of nature' that were supposedly true in some absolute sense – and the private world, whose preoccupation was to be morality, values, opinions, and religion. Prior to this time, these two aspects of human existence had always been integrated. In economic terms, the means of production in the home had been indispensable to the marketplace where goods were bought and sold – while it had been taken for granted that religious and moral values had universal validity which encompassed the public world of politics and economics just as much as the world of personal behaviour. But now all this changed. With the growth of capitalism and the concept of the market, any sense of mutuality between the home and the public world soon disappeared. Instead of the family serving as the basic unit of economic production, work was centralized and mechanized in such a way that all significant economic activity had to take place in the organized industrial context of factories and the associated activities that became necessary to resource and fuel them. Within a very short time, access to the public world of employment and economic production was the sole preserve of men, while the domestic world in the home became the place where women found their role in life.

The traditional family function of providing its members with economic support, employment, education and socialization was taken over by outside agencies. Once the family no longer had a productive economic function, it inevitably became the consumer of goods from elsewhere. With such a massive displacement of the original purposes of the family, it became necessary to redefine its function in the new circumstances, and that amounted to spelling out the roles to be played by the various members of the family circle. From now on, men were to be fathers and providers, while women were to be devoted wives, offering support and nurture, and childhood would be an age of innocence. Patriarchy was institutionalized, and the male public world became all-important. Of course, the female private world still had its function, but even that was determined by the needs of the public world. Out of this arose the image of a man going out to do battle on behalf of his family, and then retreating into the home at day's end to be revived by the caring attentions of his wife. For her part, the wife would also in due course find herself redefined as a major consumer of marketable goods. In addition, since values and faith had been relegated to the private world of the home which, by definition, was not the place where men did anything productive (that male role having been located exclusively in the public world, which by definition was also considered to be non-religious), she would also become the primary (even sole) provider of moral and spiritual guidance for her children.

All this reflected the prevailing philosophy of the day, in which everything was organized in accordance with the scientific models of people like Francis Bacon (1561-1626) and Isaac Newton (1642–1727). There needed to be an explanation for everything, with everything in its orderly place and a neat theory of cause and effect to explain it all. In human terms, this meant it was very important to know where everyone fitted in. Social class assumed a new significance, and the preservation of appropriate boundaries and demarcation lines was a priority. Indeed, by identifying this neat rational process with so-called 'laws of nature' that were believed to be built into the very foundation of the cosmos itself, anything that fitted this paradigm was therefore by definition 'right', because that was the way the universe itself had been made to function. By the same token, anything that seemed to question the received wisdom could be dismissed as non-rational, and therefore of little consequence.

Today, that has all disappeared and the working models of modern science are taken from Einstein's theory of relativity, together with chaos and complexity theory. Yet in spite of the collapse and virtual abandonment of the previous ideological foundation of Western culture, its legacy in terms of differentiated family roles is still exceedingly strong in some circles, and continues to contribute to the misery suffered in today's changing families. It has also had a significant impact in some Christian circles, particularly in relation to defining the respective roles of women and men in the spiritual nurture of children.

Of course, the realities of life in the eighteenth and nineteenth centuries often threatened to destroy even this minimal under-standing of the family as a cohesive and mutually supportive unit. Whatever the theory, economic necessity could mean that all members of a family were forced into paid employment, including children as well as women, whether they wanted it or not. In spite of the fact that the reality was often different, ordinary working people nevertheless saw the model of the industrial nuclear family as an ideal to be aimed for, and as living standards gradually increased more and more of them were able to achieve it. By the middle of the nineteenth century, most families were organized this way. Instead of having the central role in economic production, occupied by families since the very dawn of time, the major functions of the family became the provision of emotional fulfilment for its members (to make them happy), and to form the backbone of the consumer society (even today, TV adverts abound with images of the perfect nuclear industrial family, with the subliminal message that if you buy a particular product, your family can be like the one on the screen). Governments also encouraged the growth of this kind of family as an instrument of social stability (it was recognized that men who were providers were less likely to be criminal than those who were not). And naturally there was considerable emphasis on the family as the place for the nurture of children, because no 'real' family was then seen to be complete without them: they had almost become 'possessions' again, sometimes even status symbols.

The 1940s and 1950s were probably the heyday of this style of industrial nuclear family, reflected in the kind of literature provided for children at this period, none more typical than the stories of Dick and Dora and their family which constituted the first introduction to reading for generations of British primary school children. They were the very model of children who were 'seen and not heard', while their mother was compliant and supportive, with her role in life defined exclusively by reference to the needs of the rest of her family. The reality for many families was, of course, quite different from this idealized picture. By today's standards, women were certainly exploited, spending hours in drudgery such as washing clothes with primitive implements – and probably suffering no less abuse and violence than they do today, without even the minimal protection that is now available. Nor was it all fun for men, a majority of whom spent their lives at hard physical labour in exchange for pitiful rewards, frequently dying at an early age as a direct consequence, either through industrial accidents or diseases related to the workplace. Those who survived generally found themselves locked into social class structures that offered them no chance of improving their situation, no matter how hard they worked.

However much we might romanticize the industrial nuclear family, few would wish to turn the clock back to these grim realities. Even today a disturbing number of modern families still struggle with problems that, for them, have changed little over the generations, and some of the most obvious trends of today's social scene have their origins in the legacy of the Industrial Revolution and, behind it, the philosophy of the Enlightenment.

The Post-Industrial Family

Western culture is changing faster today than at any time in recent history. Indeed, because of the ease with which information can now be exchanged, we might well be living through the fastest period of cultural change there has ever been. In the past, change tended to be a subtle business, with new generations slowly altering the way their predecessors had done things, and allowing an appropriate period of time for the changes to be integrated into people's lifestyles and understandings. Nowadays change is instantaneous and global. It has become fashionable to attach the label 'post-modernism' to today's culture, but the many conflicting meanings given to that term only serve to reinforce our impression that no-one really knows what is going on, and applying a name to it is giving us the false impression that we can somehow control it all. Whatever it is, post-modernity is a familiar condition to us all. We have a love-hate relationship with the industrial and technological age that emerged from the Enlightenment. No-one would wish to turn the clock back, but neither are we all completely happy with our heritage. As a result, we struggle to make sense out of the discontinuities and contradictions, and nowhere is this more obviously true than in the family. In this context, we are faced with three major issues whose roots are deeply embedded in Western culture itself.

New Values

One of the major changes stemming from this period has been the emergence of a technological, or technocratic society. A central feature of such a society is the belief that all human needs are technical in nature. Inevitably, technical needs require specialists and experts to understand them, who then translate basic human needs into economic programmes, management procedures, and pieces of merchandise. There is no shortage of evidence for this understanding of life, and its widespread adoption lies at the heart of much contemporary dissatisfaction with Western culture. It has been responsible for the personal alienation many now feel and, ultimately, has also played a significant part in the developing environmental crisis. The technocratic outlook leads to a very narrow definition of what constitutes 'value', with anything that is 'natural' being regarded as of no value at all, including the family. Edward Goldsmith has expressed it succinctly:

It is fundamental to the world-view of modernity that all benefits are man-made – products of scientific, technological and industrial progress, made available via the market system. Thus health is seen as something that is dispensed in hospitals . . . with the aid of the latest technological devices and pharmaceutical preparations. Education is seen as a commodity that can only be acquired from schools and universities . . . *natural benefits – those provided by the normal workings of biospheric processes*, assuring the stability of our climate, the fertility of our soil, the replenishment of our water supplies, *and the integrity and cohesion of our families and communities – are not regarded as benefits at all; indeed, our economists attribute to them no value of any kind. It follows that to be deprived of these non-benefits cannot constitute a 'cost' and the natural systems that provide them can therefore be destroyed with economic impunity.*[7]

With the dominance of this kind of outlook, no-one should be surprised that the essential nurturing function of the family as a place of safety, security and personal and spiritual growth for those who live within it has been marginalized as being no longer a worthy objective. Yet historically the family has played a key role in the socialization of its members and the development of their ability to forge appropriate relationships with others, both within and outside the home context.

Economic Realities
Historically, the second major responsibility of the family has been as an economically productive unit, and the nature of work undeniably continues to play a decisive part in affecting today's family lifestyles,

in two ways. One is the obvious fact that women are now a significant part of the employed workforce, alongside men. The other is the fact that the nature of work itself is changing. Both of these are having a major impact on the family. There is no doubt that many good things have been achieved in the world of paid work during the course of this century. Though in many ways the Industrial Revolution actually made women's lives harder, this period also sowed the seeds of their ultimate empowerment, and when the need for workers in the marketplace was accentuated by the absence of men during World War I, the trend to exclude women from productive work was reversed for all time.[8]

The invention of labour-saving devices for housework in the 1950s, together with the development of reliable contraception in the 1960s, opened up new possibilities for both men and women. But ironically the sense of freedom has been short-lived. By the 1980s, what had seemed like a new freedom had been transformed by rising inflation into economic necessity, which made it impossible for most homes to live on only one income, and actually required that all the adults in a family should be engaged in paid employment. Yet paradoxically, at the very same time the nature of work had itself been undergoing radical change. In Britain in the 1970s 90% of all those who were in paid employment worked for an organization of some kind. By the early 1990s, that figure was just over 50%. This is having some far-reaching repercussions for families. Those people who still work as employees in organizations are finding that there are fewer of them, and they are having to work harder. They may be getting more money, but they are often having to work hours that are bad for relationships, and therefore for families. Only 30% of British workers now work a 'standard' 9–5 day, and the rest are having to fit their lives around working hours that are being re-organized not for their benefit, but for the good of their employing institutions. Working a 70-hour week wears people out, and can have serious social implications. In Japan, for instance, which has one of the most intense working weeks in the world, the birth-rate has fallen to only 1.1 per female, which is half the number required to sustain a stable population. On top of this, many more people have no work, or insecure part-time or temporary employment. No work and too much work are equally bad for families.

At the same time, the reorganization of work is not all bad news. The emergence of so-called designer lifestyles in which people set up their own portfolio of work, selling a product or a service, rather than their own time, offers a new and potentially beneficial space for dealing with the many conflicting pressures faced by today's families, as it gives people more flexibility in the way they use their time and therefore more opportunities to be available to their family in different ways at different stages of their life. Moreover, it is not a lifestyle that need be restricted to only one social class. It is as easy for a joiner or a plumber to have a portfolio of different kinds of work as it is for a lawyer or an accountant, and the resultant flexibility might yet have a positive effect on families as we enter the next century.[9]

Individualism

The one thing that may hinder any positive development is yet another legacy from the Enlightenment, namely a stress on individualism. The Enlightenment elevated human reason almost to a godlike status, and laid great emphasis on individuals having free choice. In the event, the choices available to them turned out to be no more free than they had ever been, because the options were always closely defined by technological and bureaucratic structures. But the resultant mind-set that put people and their individual needs and choices first is still deeply engrained in most people who, faced with several possibilities, will generally choose the one which has most in it for them. This is one issue on which Christians should have a distinctive outlook, following the teaching of Jesus that 'It is more blessed to give than to receive' (Acts 20:35).

The irony is that the thing most people seem to be searching for today is a place to belong and to be accepted. With all our concern for individual freedoms, no-one seems to know who they are any longer. The post-modern *angst* of which we hear so much is essentially a crisis in personal identity. On the dust-jacket of his

best-selling book *Life After God*, Douglas Coupland asks 'How do we
cope with loneliness? How do we deal with anxiety? The collapse of
relationships? How do we reach the quiet, safe layer of our lives?'[10]
None of these questions will ever be addressed on an individual
basis, for they are all relational questions.

These questions are not confined to dysfunctional families. Even in
those families which appear to be making it, many men find themselves struggling to redefine their personal identity in the light of
changes in family structures. Women find themselves not set free by
the changing patterns of work and economic interdependence, but
instead are struggling with a new form of enslavement, as they
wrestle with two jobs instead of one. Many children are faced with
the reality of their own vulnerability both within the home, as
victims of violence and abuse, and beyond it as they wonder what
might happen to them should the family disintegrate. In addition to
that, there are growing numbers of non-family homes, including
increasing numbers of single people as well as couples with no children. All these groups face their own unique challenges, and there
are no simple answers or quick fixes for any of them. As a culture,
we will only begin to face up to the crisis that confronts us when we
recognize the importance of community and go on from there to find
new models for community living in the light of today's new circumstances. For generations past, the family has provided people with
their first experience of living in community. It is therefore
inevitable that the fragmentation of the family will have wider social
repercussions. That is the sense in which families are the building
blocks of society. Consequently if our families are consistently
malfunctioning, then our entire civilization could well be in danger.
The renewal of the vitality of our culture will depend to a significant
extent on our ability first to visualize and then to create new models
of family that will take what is best from the past and match that
with the social realities of life at the beginning of a new millennium.
That enterprise provides both a challenge and an opportunity for the
Christian Church.

2

WHO ARE TODAY'S FAMILIES?

Given the enormous upheaval and change currently being experienced in Western culture, it is no surprise that the family is in a state of flux. The adult members of today's families wrestle with challenges that would have been unthinkable in their grandparents' generation. It is not just that their answers would have been different from ours: for the most part, they would not even understand the pressing issues that are now forcing so many people to ask fundamental questions about what we really want the family to be.[1]

It is easy to become paranoid about this, but we need to keep it in perspective. Family life has never been straightforward. How could it be, when it has involved interpersonal relationships in all times and cultures? Every kind of human relationship is open to squabbles and disagreements that can result in the breakdown of mutual understanding on either a temporary or a permanent basis. The more intimate the relationship, the greater is the potential for both good and ill within it. Ecstasy and agony can be experienced in equal measure in the family, and in most families both extremes are taken for granted as part of the ongoing personal growth that hopefully arises out of all such relationships. When the agony seems to exceed the ecstasy more often than not, then something has to give. When the parameters of society's understanding of the relationship itself are changing, it is harder still to try to make sense of things, because there is no accepted norm of what it is that we are supposed to be aiming at. Yesterday's families faced the struggle within the context of a clear notion of what constituted a family. Today's families are also striving to redefine what it means to be a family, and in that context even quite straightforward problems of relationship become exceedingly complex and, in personal terms, life-threatening – in a metaphorical sense for many, and even in a literal sense for an increasing minority.

By comparison with the past, modern families are generally smaller, with fewer children, and all the relationships (between parents, between parents and children, and between children themselves) are a good deal less stable than they were two generations ago. Single-parent families are a growing phenomenon, which now account for 20% of all British families, while there are more non-family homes than ever before, including increasing numbers of single people as well as couples who either choose to have no children or are unable to do so. All these changes – and others – are manifestations of much bigger shifts that are happening in our entire culture, and they are leading to the emergence and acceptance of many new forms of family, as people struggle to make sense out of it all.

We can trace at least seven quite distinct types of family in Western culture today.[2] In later chapters we will be looking in more detail at how the Church can support people in these varied lifestyles. But first it will help to have a bird's-eye view of the whole family landscape.

1 Husband-and-Wife Families

This is, if you wish, the traditional family style, with two married parents living together, along with those children who are biologically related to them. In cultural terms its modern evolution has been deeply affected by the Enlightenment and Industrial Revolution, while in relational terms Christians would point to the teaching of Jesus, especially his endorsement of the monogamous lifelong commitment of one man and one woman to each other, as providing some kind of normative expectation that this sort of family will try to fulfil. Even within this one model of family life, however, there are several possible variations, and it will come as no surprise to realize that these variations are related to the role of the family as an economic unit, and the changing nature of work.

In many families, both parents will be in full-time paid employment that takes place outside the home. The major incentive for this is likely to be economic necessity: unless one partner has extraordinary earning power, or either or both has inherited wealth, then most people find it simply is not possible to survive on only one income.[3] Poverty (which is always relative, of course) creates its own problems, and though many people say they would rather be poor and happy, given the chance most of us would prefer to be financially secure as a first priority. After all, the viability of the family as an economic unit has always been one of the prime functions of a family. But achieving this understandable aim does not come cheap, and has its own impact on another important purpose of family life, namely the promotion of secure, stable and nurturing relationships.

Adults cannot avoid conflicts as they try to balance the demands of two jobs alongside their family obligations. They are in turn required to be parent, partner, career worker, and domestic worker – or more accurately, they need to be all four at the same time, which is never easy. Given that today's parents of young children tend to be older than their counterparts in previous generations, they might easily be called at the same time to play a fifth family-related role as well, that of carer for their own ageing parents. Squeezed at so many different points, it is easier to talk of personal growth and fulfilment than it is actually to achieve it. Into the bargain, even those who appear to succeed in this complex balancing act frequently harbour unresolved doubts about the impact their pressurized lifestyle is likely to have on the development of their children. They find themselves struggling to locate adequate and affordable care for their children (at least in their early years), but even when they find it they are probably going to feel more or less guilty about handing over so much of the nurture of their offspring to someone else, who may or may not share their own sense of standards and values. When politicians and social service agencies assume that the ideal is for all adults to be in full-time paid employment, but at the same time insist that the major responsibility for raising children lies with parents, it is predictable that many people will go through this stage of life convinced of their own inadequacies, and with enormous problems of guilt building up that can easily afflict them for the rest of their lives.

Not all husband-and-wife families find that both partners either wish, or are able, to work full time outside the home. There are still many in which the husband is the only wage-earner. To those who struggle with the pressures of juggling home and outside work, it can often seem as if these people must have it a lot easier. The truth is they face their own challenges as well. Women in such families often find themselves put down and misunderstood even by their friends. For generations such women have been referred to as 'housewives', a term which in itself is demeaning and depersonalizing, implying that their lives are concerned with serving inanimate objects (houses) rather than working in partnership with other persons (husbands). The use of the term 'homemaker' is a more accurate (and affirming) description of the lifestyle of women who choose to be full-time partners and parents instead of taking up outside paid employment, but in Britain there is still some way to go on this issue, especially in churches. When we have used this term in seminars, we have often been accused of being 'trendy'. But it is not about trendiness for its own sake. The language we use expresses our attitudes, and in this case we need to choose our words carefully so they communicate the values of God's kingdom, which (among other things) are about lifting people up and affirming their worth, not putting them down.

Being called a 'housewife' can be bad enough. But to be asked the question, 'Do you work?' (often expressed that way in all innocence by those who take it for granted that 'work' means paid employment) can be an even more provocative and demeaning experience, and unless they take specific steps to develop their assertion skills, such women are likely to go along with the prevailing tide and admit that they do not 'work' – even though they probably put in at least a twelve–hour day in the family home. It is but one of many ironies in society's attitudes to the family that the only people who give a value to work within the home are insurance companies paying out on life policies. On their current estimates, in Britain a full-time home-maker is worth about £18,000 a year to the family budget. Not many women who choose to stay at home and raise children feel worth that much. The majority feel undervalued by society, and as a result suffer from a low self-esteem, which later in life may inhibit them from exploring other avenues of self-fulfilment, because of their lack of confidence in their own abilities.

Paradoxically, many men also find that being the sole provider in a family places enormous burdens on them. The economic stress of having both partner and children dependent on them can be quite devastating, and sometimes life-threatening. Especially in North America, men in this position often find themselves forced to take on two or three part-time positions, as well as their full-time paid employment, just to make ends meet. They literally work them-selves to death. Those men who choose to be the sole provider because they hold to a patriarchal ideology which cannot counten-ance the prospect of their wives taking paid employment will have additional pressures, most notably through competition for jobs and promotion from women in the workplace, which they find ideologi-cally unacceptable and personally threatening. Managing to solve the day-care problem by having one parent give up work outside the home can have far-reaching knock-on effects in other areas of life which impact the dynamic of family life every bit as much as having two partners in paid employment. Many Christians find themselves caught up in this particular dilemma.

This does not exhaust the possibilities for husband-and-wife fam-ilies. In other circumstances, families find either that the wife is the only one with paid employment outside the home, or that neither adult partner is working. Some people choose this as an option, and agree by mutual consent that the woman will take outside employment while the man becomes what is inaccurately referred to as a 'house husband' (just like the woman who chooses to work in the home, a man in this position is also entitled to be valued positively as a homemaker). At one stage of our married life, we ourselves lived this way. In practice, this course of action tends to be open only to those with a good deal of underlying economic stability in life, certainly in those countries (like Britain) which resist the provision of paternity leave from full-time paid employment. But it is not without its problems. Many of the self-help groups that have proliferated for the support of parents with young children are organized on the assumption that it is the mother who will care for them. Even the most self-confident man will not find it easy to join a mother and toddler group, or to find a safe place to change a baby's clothes in the bathroom facilities at shopping malls, while a visit to a health-care clinic can be equally problematic if the facilities are set up on the assumption that only women and children will be using them.

In most families where the wife is the sole earner, this situation is brought about unintentionally through economic deprivation, usually triggered by the husband losing full-time employment. In families where both parents have been earning, the wife naturally continues to do so (though with renewed intensity), while in those where the wife was not previously employed in paid work, the increasing availability of part-time jobs, many of which are geared to the recruitment of women (and poorly paid) may have to provide the only financial lifeline for the family. When it is caused by underlying poverty, families in which the woman is the only one in paid employment face the same pressures as those where neither adult has paid work. Partners who find themselves forced into spending more time together without adequate financial resources suffer increasing levels of stress, which all too often can lead to personal frustration, and spill over into violence and eventual breakdown within the family.

2 Single-Parent Families

Just as husband-and-wife families come in several different forms, so single-parent families can be divided into two very obvious categories, namely those headed by women and those headed by men.

There is some debate as to how long single parent families have been around. It can be made to seem that the number of single-parent families has increased markedly during recent years, but that has to be balanced against the fact that prior to 1967 in the UK the government never collected any statistics under this heading. In fact, the phenomenon as such is not a recent innovation, and many women in previous generations found themselves single-handedly bringing up children: husbands were killed in wars, they migrated leaving their families behind, they deserted their wives and just disappeared. There was always unmarried pregnancy as well, and the persistent fact that men have a shorter life expectancy than women.

Very few people set out with the intention of creating a one-parent family, though there is a discernible trend in this direction, especially among professional women who want to have babies but are not interested in long-term relationships. But single-parent families generally come about either by the death of a spouse or as a result of divorce. In the past, partners who hit on hard times in their relationships either resolved their difficulties, or reached an understanding to live separate lives while sharing the same home, or accepted a deteriorating domestic situation characterized by violence and hostility simply because in economic terms there was no alternative, at least not for women. Changes in the nature of available work have now altered all that − at least in theory − and the possibility of living independently, coupled with new divorce laws, have been major factors in the increasing number of single-parent families.

Women as Single Parents

Not all single-parent families are poor, but the vast majority are. Most single women bringing up children by themselves are living below the generally accepted poverty level, and need to rely on some form of state assistance in order to survive at all. This fact is so obviously indisputable that in many situations being a single woman and a parent is synonymous with poverty – the 'feminization of poverty' as it is often called. The reasons are not hard to comprehend. If it is difficult for families with two parents to juggle successfully with all the demands of modern life, then for many lone parents it is virtually impossible. When it comes to finding employment, all the dice are stacked against them, and it is exceedingly difficult to get jobs that are financially worthwhile in the short term, or that have any long-term prospects. Most employers demand 100% commitment to the job – something that, by definition, single parents find even harder to give than those who are living with a partner. In any case, many single parents are relatively unskilled, often because they have committed themselves wholeheartedly to marriage at an early age, and as a result it is only poorly paid or casual work that is available to them.

They also face other problems. On a personal level they frequently suffer from intense loneliness, lacking any resources for emotional and sexual fulfilment, and unable to create space to forge new and meaningful adult relationships because of the time commitment demanded by their (often young) children – not to mention the attitudes of other people who can still be hopelessly patronizing and unsupportive. Even when a single female parent does manage to find work she can expect to find herself subjected to unfair discrimination, and to verbal and sexual harassment, by men who see her as easy game and married women who feel threatened by her lifestyle. Many women also live with the ever-present threat of physical violence from the previous spouse, not to mention other men who will always be looking for temporary relationships. Even when new relationships are formed, without adequate commitment to the children they can be unhelpful at best, and stressful – even destructive – at worst.

Men as Single Parents

Single-parent families headed by men always come into being as a result of the death of a spouse or divorce. Generalizations can be misleading, but on the whole single fathers seem to have an easier life than single mothers. For one thing, men are usually economically better off than women. In addition, because of the way childcare decisions are taken in the courts, they are usually parenting older children. This presents its own challenges, of course, but caring for older children is a different and, on the whole, less intensive commitment (certainly in time) than caring for toddlers. As children grow up they do not need attention for 24 hours a day, they can feed and wash themselves, they are usefully occupied in school – and they are also capable of accepting responsibility for some of the everyday tasks that need to be done about the home.

Statistically, men also tend to stay single for shorter periods than women. But they have many problems in common with single female parents: finding adequate day care for children, personal loneliness, social isolation, a lack of emotional and sexual fulfilment, plus all the conflicting demands of career, housework and parenting with which families of all types must wrestle.

The attitudes of society at large toward families headed by single men can vary enormously. Sometimes friends and neighbours will be extraordinarily protective, sharing meals and services with single fathers in a way they would never dream of doing for a single mother. On the other hand, single male parents can find themselves unfairly subjected to suspicion about their motives. Social workers are tempted to imagine that any man living alone with children must by definition spend most of his time abusing them, either physically or sexually or both. Why else would a man want to bring up children alone? That kind of question is not often addressed to single female parents, and when men are faced with such hostility (on top of all the other pressures of single parenthood) they are inclined to distance themselves as far as possible from the social services, which in turn effectively cuts them off from some of the assistance that might, in theory, be available to help them and their children cope.

3 Changing Families

Most families do not exactly fit any of the previous models on a long-term basis. As time passes, families change, and a majority of people anticipate that and plan for it. No-one can be a full-time parent for ever, because children grow up and their parenting needs change, which inevitably affects the lifestyle of the whole family. Most parents would probably hope that one of them could be a full-time parent while their children are small, but would not regard that as a permanent situation, and would expect to resume paid employment outside the home on a progressive basis as circumstances changed. In the short term, harsh economic realities often make it difficult or impossible for people to fulfil this aspiration. They simply cannot survive following the expiry of a statutory period of paid parental leave from work immediately after the birth of a child, and as a result they are forced to return to full-time employment sooner rather than later, regardless of what their personal preferences might otherwise be. In any case, it is not always easy for a parent to plan to return to work some years in the future. The nature of particular jobs might undergo radical change in the meantime, necessitating retraining, and there are very few careers where it is possible to take several years out and then return to the same rung on the promotion ladder. There is a major social challenge here for governments. If we want to have enough babies to renew the population, while providing families with lasting economic security and supporting people's expectations of having meaningful paid employment, then there will need to be appropriate provision to enable that to happen.

4 Blended Families

Like the single-parent family, step-parenting is not a new phenomenon. Parents faced with the loss of their partner, for a variety of reasons, have always been inclined to remarry, and have then faced the prospect of trying to help children who are not directly related to one another to live harmoniously in the same family. But the form this takes nowadays is much more complex than it was in the past, and with increasing levels of divorce and remarriage, more and more parents find themselves faced with the task of trying to blend together children from different relationships so as to form a new, cohesive family unit. The fact that this is happening at all says something important about the way the family is regarded as being fundamental to human welfare and happiness. The breakdown of one set of relationships is not leading to the death of the family, but to its reorganization. Being a step-parent is itself a major challenge for anyone, but the more children that are involved the more difficult it becomes. It can take years for husband and wife to blend their own pre-existing families into a new social unit, and if in the meantime new children are born out of their own relationship with each other, that merely adds a further dimension to the problem.[4]

Churches find it hard to relate to blended families. Some will not countenance remarriage after divorce under any circumstances. Others want to have it both ways, and refuse to remarry people, while still recognizing such marriages as valid. Either way, families in this situation can get the impression that there is no place for them in the Church. Some time ago we were involved in the formation of a church parenting group, the story of which is documented more fully in chapter 7. It was interesting to hear parents talk about their own families. One couple described themselves as a near-perfect example of the industrial nuclear family. But after hearing the stories some of the rest of us told, the man of this particular partnership indicated that he wanted to say more. He went on to reveal that the family he had first mentioned was not his only family. He also had other children from a previous relationship, and they had subsequently been blended into a new family with their mother and her new partner. It was interesting that it took him some time to feel that Christians could provide a safe enough environment for him to talk along these lines: his initial impression was obviously that, however important it all was to him, he needed to keep quiet about such things if he was to find acceptance in the Church. As it happened, this particular situation was fairly straightforward, as his present wife had no previous children. But others might be wrestling with blending one family together, while also trying to be an absentee parent to other children who are blending in a different home. This kind of scenario is likely to be increasingly common in the future, and it raises profound conflicts for the parents and children who are involved.

Internal competition within the parents' own relationship can be a major stress in blended families, with unaddressed emotional baggage to sort out, as well as new styles of relationship to be developed with former spouses. But there will also be different levels of relationships within the new home, and in that context the predictable problems of all parenting are likely to be magnified, with increased problems of sibling rivalry, competition for the parents' attention and emotional manipulation of one group by the other, not to mention conflicts over who receives discipline from whom. Some children in such circumstances might even openly try to wreck the new family, seeing it as the cause of all their problems, rather than a possible way out of them.[5]

In principle, the extended family circle should be able to help out here. But in reality, in-laws are often a big problem anyway, and the more sets of them there are to deal with (as grandparents, if not strictly in-laws), the more complex and problematic the situation can be. Nevertheless, when this kind of intergenerational care is exercised with sensitivity for the needs of both parents and children, it can provide stability and continuity that will support the personal development of both. On the other hand, for many couples trying to blend families together, the hassle is just not worth the effort and they are cast back on their own resources as they try to cope.

5 Cohabiting Families

This kind of family appears in different versions, though they are all variations on the husband–and–wife family and the blended family. Many of the general observations made under those headings will also apply here. Cohabitees face exactly the same difficulties of balancing full-time paid employment, parenting, housework, and so on as do their married counterparts. They wrestle with the same kind of economic problems, not to mention domestic violence, which is something that threatens all family relationships. The only really distinctive feature is that this family has a differently structured relationship between the parents, who instead of getting married have chosen to live together unmarried. Even here, though, there is more than one reason why people choose to do so. For many, it is a short-term measure forced upon them by the fact that they are still married to other people, and it is not possible to remarry until divorce proceedings have been finalized. Others, though technically free to marry, choose to cohabit for a period in order to ascertain whether the relationship is likely to work out in the longer term. Yet others find themselves forging cohabiting relationships on a temporary basis, while their main ongoing family style is that of single parent.

It is easy for Christians to take a negative attitude toward all this. But the fact is that neither marriage, nor faithfulness in marriage, is dying out. Many cohabiting relationships display an extraordinary degree of fidelity, and last longer than many marriages. In addition, most cohabiting relationships do in any case eventually lead to marriage. Whether that will continue depends on a variety of social and economic factors. At the upper end of the scale, couples may find that it is to their economic advantage to form relationships based on formal legal contracts, rather than on marriage as understood by civil legislation. That way, they can ensure an equitable and mutually agreed distribution of their wealth in the event of a breakdown. At the lower end of the income bracket, people can actually find themselves economically disadvantaged by being married. According to a 1995 report from Britain's Institute of Economic Affairs, current childcare legislation in the UK means that a single mother with two small children can work for 20 hours a week at £4 an hour and end up with a net weekly income of £163 after paying tax and rent, whereas a married father of two small children working for 40 hours at the same rate would end up with £130 – £33 less for working full time than the mother does for part-time work. In the words of the report, 'What sort of message is this sending out to young people who are planning their lives? Instead of encouraging them to think in terms of making a permanent commitment to a partner in order to bring up children in a stable environment, we seem to be saying to them, "Don't get married". For many people, especially at the bottom of the earnings scale, marriage has become an unaffordable luxury.'[6]

6 Couples Without Children

In view of all that has been said so far in this chapter, you might think that an obvious resolution for many of the problems would be for adults to choose to have no children. Since most of the tensions identified in family life relate to the problem of balancing the needs of adult relationships with those of children, then presumably being childless removes a major obstacle to the achievement of human happiness. But life is not that simple, and one of the reasons we have chosen to include childless homes here as a possible type of 'family' is that for some couples the absence of children creates at least as many problems as their presence does for others.

Some couples voluntarily choose to be childless. No Western country has yet followed the example of China which for economic reasons tries to limit every couple to just one child. But they don't need to, as the economic pressures of affluence can have a similar effect. For couples where both partners are engaged in fulfilling work, progressing steadily along clearly-defined career tracks with rising expectations of both personal fulfilment and financial prosperity, the whole system is geared up to persuading them either to delay having children for as long as is physically possible or (what often amounts to the same thing, by default) never having them at all. Considerations motivating such choices include the probability that the woman will never be able to regain her position in career terms after the birth of a child, no matter how short a leave she takes from paid employment, as well as the fact that both of them are probably having to work so hard that they literally would have no time to fulfil a parenting role in any adequate fashion.

When those who have work are being forced into longer and longer hours, the pressure on couples to decide to remain childless is increasing all the time. For instance, when John started teaching in a British university twenty years ago, it was an employment situation that was very family-friendly. There was a specified amount of work that needed to be done, and that formed the basis on which university teachers were paid. Within that framework there was considerable flexibility. Today, that has disappeared. Not only are teachers in British higher education being expected to work longer hours – including in some cases evening and weekend work as well as work during what would otherwise be vacation periods – but they are also being pressurized to produce quality research publications, for the execution of which most institutions are either unwilling or unable to provide time or facilities within the parameters of what might be regarded as an ordinary working week of 40–45 hours. As a result, many academics find that the only way to fulfil all their employer's expectations is to work long hours, and the only way to do that is to cut down on time spent with families. Their choice is stark: either they spend all their evenings and weekends doing the research work for which there is no time–provision in the working week, and thereby lose out on quality time spent with their family; or they choose different priorities in the home, and thereby lose out on promotion in the workplace. This scenario is by no means unique to academic life. It is rapidly becoming the norm for many people, and not just those in so-called professional occupations. With ever longer opening hours in shops, factories, and offices – all of them organized for the benefit of the institutions, not for the personal convenience of the staff - is it any wonder that more and more people are making a choice to remain childless? They simply have enough to do already, without adding to their busy lives the demands of parenthood. Indeed, many of them are too tired to have sex for any purpose whatever.

In social terms, no-one yet knows where this trend will lead, but in almost all Western nations the present birth rate is insufficient to renew the population, even in the medium-term. When so many people who would be otherwise well equipped to raise mature people for the future choose not to do so, that is bound to have far-reaching repercussions for the whole shape and balance of the culture of future generations. Precisely because they are aware of such considerations, many couples who choose to be childless often suffer from guilt for the rest of their lives, always wondering whether or not they have done the 'right' thing.

In addition, though, many couples are involuntarily childless, for a whole collection of physiological reasons. Far from finding this a blissful state, they too are under stress. In terms of their own self-image, they feel inadequate: they can never be one of those 'perfect families' so beloved of TV advertisers – so how can they be whole persons? They inevitably find themselves apportioning 'blame' for their childless state, which can easily prove to be the death blow to a relationship. And if they survive all that, they are probably still faced with angry relatives who feel they have been deprived of their rights because they have no grandchildren, nieces or nephews. Given the constraints of space, we will not say much more on the subject of couples without children in this book. But that is not a sign of indifference to their needs, which ought to be taken more seriously by the Church than they typically are.

7 Other Homes

Finally, there are a number of other possible forms of family structure of which we can make only brief mention. Single-person homes are increasing in number today. People become single for a variety of reasons. Some just grow from adolescence into adulthood without forging lasting relationships with someone they might marry. But increasing numbers of people are finding their marriages break up not when their children are still young, but after they have left the family home. As a result, they too become single people, rather than being single parents in the technical sense of the word. It seems inevitable that over the next few years many of these single-person homes will also become family homes, at least on a short-term basis, as increasing numbers of single people, with no children of their own to care for, offer to serve as foster parents, or even to adopt children as a long-term commitment.

There is also an emerging family model based on gay relationships, both between homosexual men and lesbian women. As the law stands at the moment in Britain, there is no reason in principle why gay couples should not foster and adopt children, while increasing numbers of lesbian women are opting for short-term liaisons with men in order to conceive children, but with no intention other than raising those children within the context of their own long-term gay relationship. This is another topic which space does not allow us to discuss in detail, except to observe that such family units are a social reality and if Christians are not to abdicate all responsibility for the family, then we will have to consider how best to meet their particular needs.[7]

In addition, variations on the extended family home are becoming more common in some contexts. For example, there is an increasing trend for grandparents to have custody of their grandchildren, on either a short- or long-term basis, especially in families where the parents have their own relationship difficulties. Such arrangements can provide a stopgap measure while parents sort out their own problems, and within the wider family circle are frequently seen as a way of handling breakdown internally, thereby avoiding the involvement of social services and the consequent possibility of children being taken into care or into foster homes. On a more permanent basis, custodial grandparenting can be very successful, but evidence shows it can also be stressful, for grandparents as well as children.[8]

The family is clearly in the midst of enormous upheaval and change. Even within the categories we have identified here, changes are still going on, which makes it difficult to forecast what the future may bring. It might well be that new versions of the extended family of the past could provide a new way forward for the future, this time not based on kinship in the strict sense, but on networks of unrelated friends and associates as well as those bound together by genetic links. Whatever the future may hold, the redesigned family will certainly feature in it. But the shape of the new design is not yet clear, nor will it be for some time to come. As a culture we are still at the drawing-board stage. The question for Christians is whether we can think big enough to make a positive contribution to this process. It is easy to say that the family today is in crisis, but that is merely to state the obvious. The Chinese have two characters which define the concept of 'crisis'. One spells 'danger', and the other means 'opportunity'. For Christians to focus on the danger, and to be constantly decrying the disappearance of the traditional Western industrial nuclear family, is the way of death. To see the situation as an opportunity will require careful discernment to enable us to identify those new emerging values that reflect God's will (and in spite of much confusion, there are plenty of signs of hope), and to work alongside other people of goodwill to ensure that these values make a positive contribution to the new image of the family that will take our descendants safely through the next century.

3

BEING A CHILD IN THE MODERN FAMILY

A child who lives with criticism learns to condemn.
A child who lives with hostility learns to fight.
A child who lives with ridicule learns to be shy.
A child who lives with shame learns to feel guilty.

A child who lives with tolerance learns to be patient.
A child who lives with encouragement learns confidence.
A child who lives with praise learns to appreciate.
A child who lives with fairness learns justice.
A child who lives with security learns to have faith.
A child who lives with approval learns to like themselves.

If children live with acceptance and friendship,
they learn to find love in the world.

Most readers of this book will be familiar with that poem. We have been unable to trace its origins, but its title, *Children Learn What They Live*, expresses succinctly some fundamental truths about human development. Who we become as adults is to a very large extent shaped by our experience as children. While it is by no means impossible for people to change direction in later life, doing so almost always involves a lot of painful heart-searching and sorting out the baggage of our childhood past. Childhood has a profound and lasting effect on adult people, for good and for ill. For a start, about

50% of a person's cognitive development takes place by the time they reach 3-4 years old.[1] But more significantly, the way children develop a self-image depends on their interaction with adults, both their parents and others who are significant in their lives. It follows that any disruption in the quality of a child's early relationships with the adults in their life is bound to have a far-reaching impact on them. In turn, anything that affects today's children is bound to have far-reaching consequences for tomorrow's adults and ultimately, therefore, for the whole shape of our communities. No-one yet knows what future effects there will be for society as a whole as a result of the difficulties faced by so many of today's children. The only certain thing is that, with increasing numbers of children having negative experiences of the family, we can expect the impact to be considerable.

Previous generations thought of their children as a contribution toward society's investment in the future. The family itself could therefore be seen as an institution that was bigger than its individual members, and for which it would be worthwhile making sacrifices and commitments that would lay solid foundations for generations yet to come. Today, many people have no hope for the future, either because they believe things are irredeemably heading for disaster or, more often, because they live only for the present and for themselves. The ambivalence with which modern Western adults treat children only reflects our own understanding of the nature of happiness. We have all been deeply affected by the individualistic philosophy of the Enlightenment, that has encouraged us to live only for ourselves, and by the technological mind-set that assumes everything can and should be delivered instantaneously. Though enormous numbers of people long to find meaningful relationships with others, very few have a concept of happiness which centres on living in community, or understands human fulfilment in terms of personal commitment and self-sacrifice. The corrosive influence of selfish individualism is widespread, and Christians are not exempt from its pervasive influence. Indeed historically the Church has played a major role in promoting it: we would do well to remember that the

Enlightenment emphasis on the autonomy of the individual ultimately had its roots in the Protestant Reformation, and the insistence that so far as God is concerned each person stands individually and personally accountable only for themselves.

We can see all this reflected today in the contradictory attitudes to children that are adopted by both individual parents and by society at large. Unlike our forebears, we do not have children for economic gain: on the contrary, they actually cost us a lot of money! Instead, we say we have children for emotional satisfaction. Paradoxically, at the same time we regularly subject them to violence and abuse of all kinds, and frequently fail to provide the stable atmosphere which will enable them to be fulfilled human beings, and which in the medium term will lead to the development of the kind of family relationships that will provide us adults with the personal satisfaction for which we claim to be desperately searching.

As a society, we say we want to provide opportunities for parents to be fulfilled through paid employment, but at the same time we refuse to make provision for their children, whether it be in terms of the structuring of employment, or in the provision of adequate day care. The problems faced by many children can be traced directly to the conflicting demands that society places upon their parents. Everyone knows the phenomenon of latchkey kids, forced to fend for themselves at an early age before and after school each day and for long hours during holiday periods. In recent years, the media (aided by Hollywood movie-makers) has highlighted the plight of children left 'home alone' while their parents take vacations. This sounds scandalous and irresponsible when expressed in that form, but the fact is that some young children are left totally unattended on a regular basis while their parents work, because no other choices are open to them. In addition, the lack of proper day care affects parents as well as children, and that can have knock-on effects in all areas of their life. Stress easily spills over into conflict both in the home and the workplace. It affects health, lowers productivity, and undermines the stability of all kinds of relationships. None of this is good for children.

Apart from the underlying tensions created by the conflicting demands society imposes on today's parents, children can find themselves in a no-win situation. On the one hand, some parents give their children absolutely no disciplinary framework whatever. By way of explanation, they say they are giving their children the freedom to develop their own lifestyles. What they are really doing is refusing to take responsibility for their children, and abandoning them to a life with no structure, limits, or values. On the other hand, they are quite likely to be making very specific demands of them, by expecting them to dress, wash and feed themselves and be responsible for their own welfare while the parents are at work. Children who are regularly left by themselves before and after school each day are bound to be more vulnerable than those who have regular adult care and supervision. The chance of getting involved in delinquency is only one manifestation of this. Many more of them are, in effect, expected to be the managers of their own home. They have to take responsibility for doing the shopping, the cleaning, and they may even be the regular cook for the entire family's evening meals. Of course, children need to be empowered to play their part in the running of the home, and it is not necessarily a bad thing for young teenagers to be expected to help clean the house, or cook for their family. But when such responsibilities are placed on children as young as seven or eight years old, and are never shared by adult family members, then children can find themselves literally enslaved in their own homes.

There is no doubt that at the present time the new emerging models of family are creating more problems than they can resolve, and they affect children in every social class. That is not to say there can be no resolution of them. But if our children are to grow up as whole and balanced people, it will require more realism about their predicament on the part of adults. The one thing that is indisputable is that children never create the circumstances in which they find themselves. It is easy to say that parents have the primary responsibility for giving their children the love and commitment they deserve and need. Governments love to say it, because they think that absolves the wider community of any responsibility. But when that wider community imposes on adults the need to be productively employed and the simultaneous need to be caring for their children, then it is essential to provide adequate support for parents who are trying to juggle so many balls at once.

One way or another, these challenges impinge on the lives of most of today's children. But they are not the only factors with which as a group they are having to contend.

Poverty

Poverty is a notoriously hard thing to define, because it is not just about economics. Whenever it is discussed, it invariably becomes a political issue. Governments are embarrassed by it and tend to play it down, while their political opponents are inclined to exaggerate it. Without getting involved in detailed political debates, we can say categorically that whereas most people in the 1970s and 1980s could expect their standard of living to improve over their working lifetime, in the 1990s we have witnessed a massive increase in poverty on a worldwide scale. Some Australian friends of ours recently visited Britain, and for their teenage son it was his first visit. He could hardly believe the number of young people he saw begging in the streets, some of them younger than he was. This was not an experience he found easy to reconcile with his image of what he thought to be British living standards. He was right: twenty years ago, most Westerners would have equated beggars with impoverished countries in the two-thirds world. Today, for a variety of reasons, homelessness and poverty are obvious facts of life in all the major towns and cities of the West. Moreover, many of the poor are *very* poor – and there are many others who, though not quite poor enough in statistical terms to be officially classed as 'below the poverty line', are still suffering significant economic deprivation.

Politicians always tackle this matter by asking who is to blame for such poverty. They argue about whether people are responsible for creating their own poverty. That is a valid question, but to address it here would divert us from our main task. For whatever the answer to that question might be, it is never children who create their own poverty. Yet more and more of them are finding their lives affected by it. A couple of generations ago, old people were the ones who were most at risk from poverty. Some still are, but in general it is children and young families who are more likely to be among the poor, especially single–parent families and two-parent families with only one adult earner.

Children can be very resilient to hardship, and even those who know they are deprived will hope for something better. But unless things do actually change, they internalize their situation and lose hope. To deprive a child of hope for the future is a form of abuse whose consequences for the rest of their life are incalculable. Is that not one of the things Jesus had in mind when he condemned so stridently those who might cause a child to lose faith (Mark 9:42)? To be a child and to have no hope is a contradiction in terms, but it is the reality for increasing numbers of children today.

Imagine if you can what life is like for a child in poor circumstances in a temperate climate: living in a damp home, missing school because of frequent illness caused by the damp and the cold, having to share a bed with your brothers and sisters, or even adults, unable to participate in all the activities at school because your parents can't afford some of them, not always having clean clothes to wear when you go to school, and never having a place at home to do homework. Hope might be kindled for a while by the promise that one day you will have better housing. But the reality is that the poor often have to move from one temporary home to another, and they can stay on waiting lists for public housing for years without anything happening. Is it any wonder that when children realize that for them there is no escape, they handle the problem either by withdrawing into their own private world, or venting their anger in delinquent activities? There seems to be a link between poverty and ill health, lower educational achievement, delinquency, and many of the other maladies afflicting children.

What is more, poverty affects the models of community living that parents can pass on to their children. Poverty can lead to violence between parents, and interminable arguments over how whatever money they have is to be spent, and who spends it. Adults caught in this situation often look to alcohol as a way of escape – and children get caught in the middle. At best, many children raised in poverty go on to repeat the cycle as adults themselves. At worst, they are forced into homelessness as teenagers and spend the rest of their lives as a liability to themselves and to the wider community.

It is tempting to make simplistic statements about the relationship between poverty and family breakdown. But it is a complex matter.[2] On the one hand, a significant factor in the increase in family poverty is certainly related to aspects of the wider family changes now taking place. For example, divorce almost invariably means a lower income for the woman, and relative poverty for her and her children. Men go their own way, and often manage to escape any kind of financial responsibility for their children. When the British government attempted to redress the balance by setting up the Child Support Agency to collect cash from fathers and redistribute it to their children and former wives, there was strenuous resistance from men who had remarried and had second or third families. They claimed that in order to meet their government-determined financial targets, their new families would be placed in jeopardy, and there would be no sense in robbing one family to pay another. The government clearly got some things wrong, for within two years of setting up the Agency they radically restructured its operations. But the nature of the underlying arguments, focusing on the perceived happiness of the various adults involved, merely served to highlight the extent to which children are the main victims of such circumstances. Nor is this a matter of social class, for even children who are born into circumstances of relative economic security can suddenly find themselves plunged into abject poverty as the result of the breakdown of their parents' relationship.

Breakdown very often creates poverty for children, but it can also work the other way round. Economic pressure itself can lead to family breakdown, and the unexpected unemployment of either or both parents can lead to problems involving violence, drugs, alcohol, and mental health. Meanwhile, the other side of the picture is that families with stable economic circumstances tend to produce well-adjusted children.

Emotions

As well as the economic consequences, divorce and separation also have a significant emotional impact on children. It is very difficult to identify a specific cause of this, as children tend to see breakdown as one major episode, whereas adults are inclined to see it as a process and therefore to compartmentalize the different elements contributing to it. It could be that it is not the divorce itself that causes emotional disturbances for children, but the tensions and pressures that precede it and the economic deprivation that often follows it. But the whole process creates major trauma. For a child, it is not just the immediate effects of separation that make a difference, but what breakdown represents in terms of their lost expectations, their broken relationships, and shattered dreams.

The negative effects of losing a parent through divorce last well beyond childhood. Role models given by parents are a vital factor in influencing a child's own later family formation, and the rise in emotional and psychological problems faced by children, not to mention the increasing incidence of teenage suicides, is all related in some way to changing support systems within the family.[3] In fact, in the medium to long term, divorce can be much harder to handle than the death of a parent. Children go through the same kind of grieving process in both instances, yet in the case of divorce there is never a final separation, which means that the agony is constantly prolonged and may never be resolved.

It is exceedingly difficult for adults to see divorce the way a child does, because their whole agenda is different. Adults divorce for many different reasons. In terms of their own life expectations, their reasons are mostly good ones – and the majority of adults divorce only reluctantly and after giving the matter much serious thought. Comedians make jokes about the 'seven–year itch', but when you think about it seven years is a significant investment of time, which itself suggests that most people only divorce after giving serious thought to all that might be involved. Children, however, find it hard to imagine that anything could possibly be important enough to be worth splitting up for. In many respects, adults' needs in a modern marriage are different from those of their children.[4] Adults are usually looking for love, fulfilment, and personal satisfaction. A child also needs love, not in terms of personal fulfilment but in the form of protection and security. For a child, to exchange those essentials for an adult's version of personal fulfilment will always seem a bad deal, or just selfishness on the part of one or both of their parents. Adults also need to remember that breakdown for a child means the loss of a person with whom they have a unique and irreplaceable relationship: you can only have one father or mother. Divorce is not without its emotional trauma for adults, but they are losing a lover, who can eventually be replaced: parents can not.[5]

In the short term, divorce has many different and unpredictable effects on children, partly related to their age when it occurs. Some suffer an overwhelming sense of loneliness and insecurity, afraid that both parents will eventually leave them. Others take sides, blaming one parent for what has happened and seeing the other one as the victim. Adolescents probably suffer the most, and their loss of security at this crucial time in their own development can create worries about whether they will be able to make relationships, or what levels of personal intimacy they can cope with. Children's immediate symptoms can be wide and varied, ranging from physical side effects such as nightmares, sleeplessness, or unexplained aches and pains, to unexpected delinquency or running away from home, or openly-expressed anger and disapproval of their parents, especially if remarriage is in view, because that means there is no chance at all of going back to the past (something that most children in divorce secretly hope for). Young adults can find their parents' divorce especially stressful, and forego any possibility of an adult relationship with them as a result. In the longer term, the trauma of divorce can affect children's own choices about relationships. They might become cynical and suspicious of marriage and less likely to want children of their own.

In helping children in such circumstances, we need to remember that we all work through our own stresses in different ways, depending on our varying temperaments and personalities. And of course children do survive the disintegration of their family. Nor should we generalize and say that in the long run divorce *per se* will always be a bad thing for a child. For a child locked in a close relationship with an abusive and violent parent, divorce can very obviously turn out to be a good thing, in the long term. But even in that situation, family breakdown is still very costly in terms of a child's emotions. Church workers called upon to advise in these situations need to be very sensitive to what is actually going on. It is too easy to advise parents to stick together at all costs – 'for the sake of the children' – while ignoring the sum total of unhappiness that such a situation perpetuates. On balance, it is probably children trapped in unhappy homes who suffer the most, but we also need to realize that children of divorce do have to handle a lot of emotional distress. We might regret that these are the only choices available to some children, but this is how it is and we need to find ways of living with it.

Violence

Physical violence can take different forms, but for many of the world's children it has become a way of life, whether experienced through starvation, disease, the ravages of war, slavery, or organized sexual exploitation. One of the most obvious facts impinging on the experience of Western children is that the family itself – the place where they have a right to expect to be given care and security – has all too often become a place of cruelty and violent oppression.

Public awareness of this has grown significantly in recent years, and it is a topic that will keep cropping up in subsequent chapters. Here we will concentrate on its impact on children. In looking at the problem, it is difficult to know whether current levels of domestic abuse and violence are one of the by-products of changing family structures, or whether things have always been like this, the only difference being that people are now more open about such things than they were in the past, and so it just seems as if violence is increasing. But it is difficult not to imagine that in many instances there must be some causal connection with other factors that are impinging on family life, because it is not just adults who perpetrate violent acts against children: there is a growing incidence of children being violent to other children. In very many of these cases their own experience of family dysfunction and breakdown plays a major part in determining the behavioural patterns of those children who engage in such violence.

Violent domestic abuse is an extremely emotive subject, and we must not fall into the trap of overstating the size of the problem. It is still only a minority of children who suffer physical abuse – but it is a bigger minority than most adults imagine, or are prepared to face up to.[6] There are different estimates of how common physical and sexual abuse is, but among researchers there is a general consensus that those cases that come to light are only the tip of the iceberg. In addition, part of the problem is a matter of definition as to what constitutes 'abuse'. For example, if children are left unattended and uncared for as a result of their parents being addicted to alcohol or drugs, then that clearly constitutes neglect – but does it also constitute abuse? Not all abuse is physical. There are many non-physical ways to abuse a child that do not involve what most people would think of as violence, but which are every bit as damaging.

Many children are consistently put down by parents and teachers, for instance, by being repeatedly told how useless they are at doing things, and how far short they fall of their parents' ideals and expectations. Religious parents are especially prone to this kind of behaviour, reinforcing their own preferences by identifying them as 'God's will', and then invoking eternal sanctions against children who fail to conform. Both of us were brought up in religious families, and suffered from this to a greater or lesser extent at different points in our childhood. At the age of eight, Olive was abandoned by her parents to the care of a foster family whom she had never met before, and who lived hundreds of miles away from all her other relatives (of whom she had very many), to free her parents to go and 'evangelize' other people's children. It took her years to work through the traumatic emotional and spiritual consequences. John has distinct memories of being told as a child of nine years old that he was the 'man of sin' referred to in various apocalyptic sections of the New Testament. Many adult Christians suffer from a lack of self-esteem as a result of similar childhood encounters – and then go on to inflict similar injustices on their own offspring.[7] The fact that Christian parents can do and say such things probably says more about the lack of support in parenting that the Church gives them than it does about their personal commitment to the welfare of their own children. Whatever the reason, many children still suffer repeatedly from verbal and psychological abuse, especially in middle-class families, because the more educated a parent is the more words they have in their arsenal with which to harm other people.

Verbal and psychological abuse are not the only problem areas. What about smacking, for example. Does that constitute violent abuse? It is certainly common, and in Britain at any rate it is not at all unusual to see a harassed parent giving a child a physical thrashing in a public place such as a shopping mall. It is also generally legal, though it is often difficult to know where to draw the line between what might constitute a legally acceptable level of physical punishment and what becomes in effect violent assault. Among Christians, some of the most heated debates on parenting centre on this issue. It is not unknown for violent men inspired by a patriarchal understanding of faith to beat not only their children, but their wives as well – sometimes justifying it in terms of 'beating the devil out of them'.

A number of factors can be identified as contributing to increasing violence in the home. We need not doubt that much domestic violence today (against women as well as children) is related to the collapse of the patriarchal family.[8] The logical outcome of belief in male domination of the family has always been that women and children are property, to be used as men wish. In the past, the logic was not always followed through in practice, and a generation or two back it may have been possible for a traditional patriarchal man to rule over his family with what might be called a benevolent sort of authoritarianism. Violence was always the ultimate sanction, but because of the acceptance of the patriarchal family, by wives as well as society at large, it was not generally necessary to exercise it. Today, that kind of man is disapproved of by society at large, and his efforts at preserving a macho image are likely to be resisted by his wife and children. It seems obvious that a man who needs to control other people in order to affirm his own identity will be threatened by all this, and is therefore likely to resort more easily to violence to try and defend his otherwise untenable position. This is no doubt one reason why violence against children and women in the home seems to be endemic in all social classes.

But it is not the only relevant consideration. There are various opinions current among the experts, but surely it stands to reason that any factors leading to a destabilizing of relationships (poverty, unemployment, stress, conflict, *etc.*) can also open the door to violence.[9] Adults' own experiences also play a part in determining their behaviour toward their own and other people's children. We know that husbands who abuse their wives also tend to abuse children, and when under pressure women who are themselves abused are more likely to inflict violence on their children. Arising out of this cycle, some families create a culture of violence in which their members know of no other way in which they can relate to one another. Then there are often other crucial parental psychological factors involved. In particular, we know that many abusers have themselves been the victims of abuse, or otherwise subjected to emotional deprivation, parental rejection and family conflict (though not everyone who suffers these things necessarily becomes an abuser). Violent parents may also be psychopaths or sociopaths, or suffer from other conditions associated with low self-esteem and high levels of insecurity.

Whatever the explanation, many children are suffering from unprovoked violence at the hands of their carers. Some end up dying either through deliberate acts of murder, or as a result of neglect. One of the most disturbing trends, however, is in the numbers of children who no longer regard the family as a place of safety and security. Many of them spend increasing amounts of time on the streets and in shopping malls, because they are safer there than at home. One result, however, is that they are vulnerable to being recruited into gangs, prostitution and other forms of delinquency and racketeering. For others, the suffering they encounter in the home is so great that they come to believe death could be a real release. Suicide is the ultimate act of hopelessness and despair, and over the last twenty years the rates among children have been rising. Some researchers suspect the true figures for child suicide are higher than the statistics suggest, because suicide as a real cause of the death of a child is hard to prove conclusively, and is also so painful for relatives to accept and cope with that police and social workers often accept incomplete explanations. Whatever the truth, a dysfunctional family is undoubtedly one of the key reasons for childhood and adolescent suicide, particularly when a child feels somehow responsible for the mess at home, and can see no way of improving it or resolving the conflict.

The crisis in the family is most keenly felt by children. They are not responsible for what is happening to them. They have not created the situations within which they have to live, and even in the most stable home situations it is easy for them to be overcome by a sense of injustice and unfairness. Of course, parents usually try their best, and at times of stress and crisis in their own relationships many people will find support from their own informal networks of relatives and friends to look after their children. But for many more, there is no way to cope and they find their children taken into care. For some children that can be the answer to their prayers. For others being in care can sometimes be as traumatic an experience as the original home situation was. If such children grow up without adequate support from their families, then as teenagers they can easily slip out of the care system, taking with them unrealistic ambitions to set up their own homes in the community, only to find they are trapped in a cycle of loneliness, unemployment and poverty. For children to be in care can only ever be a stopgap solution to particular crises. The majority of them have two possible places in which to find their identity: the street, or the family. In that situation, it makes sense to work to support the family, rather than making long-term care arrangements elsewhere, or paying the social costs of having large numbers of homeless youngsters living rough.

If we have painted a bleak picture in this chapter, then that fairly reflects how life is for huge numbers of children around the world today. But what is true for children who are obviously disadvantaged also, to some degree, reflects the problems faced by children in families that, on the surface, seem to be coping well. Church leaders in particular need to be sensitive to that fact, and adopt ministry styles that will empower children to develop as people, and to be drawn to the Kingdom of God.[10]

4

BEING AN ADULT IN
TODAY'S FAMILY

Families are built on relationships. While the precise nature of the relationships between women and men may be changing, and the acceptable diversity of family-creating adult relationships is now wider than ever before, the way in which women and men get on with each other is still fundamental to determining the basic shape of the home and facilitating the growth and development of children within it. One of the weaknesses in much thinking on the family is the way family relationships are often defined exclusively in terms of their implications for adults, without taking any account of a child's perspective. Nevertheless, the way that parents relate has a profound and inescapable impact on the life of all families. The pressures faced by women and men have a direct bearing on the experiences of children in this situation, and by identifying some of them we can pinpoint ways in which Christians can minister to one another, and help create new family structures that will be to the benefit of all who need to live within them. Some Christians believe the way women and men (and, indeed, children) relate to each other is a theological question rather than a social one. We have something to say about that aspect of the subject in our next chapter, which forms a bridge between the first part of the book, which has been more theoretical, into the second, which is more practical. Here, however, we will consider the question in terms of the everyday situations within which people have to live. Theology serves no useful purpose unless it is firmly anchored in the realities of daily life.

Women

On the face of it, women might seem to have a much easier time in today's families than their mothers and grandmothers could ever have imagined possible. The development of reliable contraception has delivered women from the rigours of having to undergo one pregnancy after another, and great advances have apparently been made empowering women to be good parents, good partners, and successful career people all at the same time. Some countries are better than others, but throughout the Western world there is no shortage of legislation aimed at making life easier and more fulfilled for women. The reality, though, is often different – sometimes very different indeed, so that in practice women can still find themselves oppressed. No amount of legislation can change the attitudes of men, or indeed of the wider culture, and even though the law may no longer officially subscribe to a patriarchal way of thinking about the relations between women and men, in practice many people still operate with that mindset, and ironically (especially within the church), women as well as men can think and behave that way.

Even among those who are self-consciously trying to redefine roles in the family, there is frequently an enormous gap between theory and reality. It is easier to pay lip service to the ideals of sharing and partnership between male and female parents than it is actually to do anything concrete about it. In terms of what actually happens in the home, women still generally find themselves expected to assume the major responsibility for what goes on there – domestic arrangements as well as the needs of children – at the same time as they are trying to hold down demanding jobs in the wider workplace.[1] In addition, women are expected to be available to help men handle their uncertainties about their own new identity in today's world, and they are usually the ones who need to handle the tensions that arise in blended families. In separation and divorce there is an almost universal expectation that it is women who should pick up the pieces, especially in relation to children and their needs. Indeed, this assumption is usually enshrined in both legislation and child-care practice.

Because of the way we have come to define 'freedom', some things that can be made to look like greater freedom for women actually have the opposite effect because of a lack of supportive resources in the wider community. For example, teenage parents are actively encouraged to raise their children as single parents in a way that certainly was not the case a couple of generations ago. There are many good reasons why, as a general principle, most reasonable people would wish to support that course of action. But in reality it does not automatically lead to freedom, nor necessarily to a greater level of happiness and fulfilment for either parents or children. All too often it results in poverty and deprivation for all concerned, and the loss of opportunities for education and self-improvement on the part of those who arguably need them most. This is a challenge for society at large, which needs to give more careful attention to the practical outworking of such double-standards, while the Church for its part ought to be more realistic about what is going on and recognize that many of those to whom it finds it hard to minister are actually being sinned-against by the very structures that, at other levels, are claiming to set them free.

All Work and No Play . . .

It is still the case that most women do most of the everyday tasks of housework, and if or when men take any responsibility they generally choose the more interesting things, or things that have typically been identified as 'men's work', in preference to the more routine and boring things like washing, ironing, and cleaning. This fundamental imbalance in home responsibilities is magnified when children are also part of the equation, because in addition it is almost invariably women who are expected to be responsible for child care, either by doing it or arranging for it. In such circumstances, women unavoidably come under stress, which itself can lead to absenteeism from work and the breakdown of physical or mental health. Mothers under stress always have a negative impact on family relationships. The 'superwoman' myth dies hard, and at one time or another probably most women try and fill this role both at work and at home.

The reality however is that a majority find themselves forced either to give up their career ambitions in some way, or to cut back on the amount of energy they invest in the home, thereby sacrificing some of their aspirations as a wife and mother.

This double – or even triple – burden borne by so many women is the most characteristic way in which today's family crisis finds expression in the average home, and it is at this point that women need most support and affirmation in their roles. The realities are stark, and choices are not easy. Many families need two earners if they are to have a decent lifestyle. In the process, women are forced to have at least two jobs, which can easily lead to stress and resentment. Most men are either unwilling to change or incapable of doing so, and as a result women are forced either to accept the pressures, or to choose divorce and single parenthood as the lesser of two evils. That analysis might sound simplistic, but give or take the odd detail, this is reality for very many women. To break out of this vicious cycle, the problem needs to be tackled at two levels.

First is the role of women and men as partners within the family. To create and maintain a successful relationship in circumstances like this, men will need to be realistic about women's needs. To put it bluntly, the way to a woman's heart, and a mutually affirming relationship, is more likely to be through washing clothes, cleaning bathrooms, ironing the washing and scrubbing the floors, than through traditional images of romantic candle-lit dinners and the like. The Church can do a good deal to promote this kind of responsible partnership. All too often congregations make unrealistic demands on the time of men in particular, which leaves them little opportunity to do their share in the home. It is not enough merely to accept that men may do their share if they wish. We should be saying loudly and clearly that it is part and parcel of a modern relationship. One way of doing that is for the Church to model partnership between women and men in its own structures, whether the leading of worship or the making of strategic decisions. Even in churches that in theory will say they have a concept of all believers ministering in partnership together, it is not uncommon to find that women still carry out only traditional roles such as child-care, cooking, and so on. People learn how to live in partnership when others model it for and with them, and churches should work hard at doing this.

Christians should also be taking a lead in asking some fundamental questions about the function of parents in bringing up children. We have already referred to the problems of self-image faced by women who want to be full-time homemakers. This is not a minority concern, for a very large number of women find themselves in this role at some stage of their lives, if only on a temporary basis. They work hard, are generally unpaid, and because they produce no 'marketable' product (at least, not as defined by the laws of strict economics), they find themselves undervalued by society as a whole. They might easily find themselves being devalued even by their friends, who see them as a free child-care service because they have 'nothing to do all day'.

In reality, the assumption that parents can find 'real fulfilment' only through paid employment outside the family context raises some far-reaching questions about mutual accountability within the family, which impinge on fathers as well as mothers. Who do we want to be providing the primary role models for our children? The parents? Or the state? Or the companies we work for? Or independent child minders? Different parents will give different answers. The same parents might easily give different answers in relation to each of their children. But, however we resolve it, there is no doubt that children who spend insufficient time with a parent at an early age are likely to have relational and identity problems in later life. The experience of those countries which provide either or both parents with paid leave from work for several months, or even longer, at the time of a child's birth seems to suggest that it is not crucial whether this care comes from fathers or mothers, or a mixture of the two. Maybe even that is scarcely radical enough. Management professor Charles Handy proposes the idea of what he calls 'time-banking', which he defines as allowing parents to take almost indefinite amounts of paid leave when their children need them, which they will make up in later life when their circumstances have changed.[2] A scheme like that would require visionary political structures. But in the medium term it might also be less costly to society as a whole. However we quantify it, there seems to be an obvious and clear connection between early negative experiences in the family and criminality and personal breakdown in later life. How can we put a value on security and loving relationships? With diffi- culty – which is why social policy all too often ignores and devalues such things. But Charles Handy (writing as a business consultant!) offers a better vision with his reminder that 'there are satisfactions and achievements which cannot be measured by money'.[3]

Working Hard for Little Reward

The economic pressures for women do not stop once they have secured paid employment outside the home. When they are in work, women are generally paid less than men, sometimes less for doing the same jobs. More often, it is only low-paid jobs that are readily available to them, for several reasons. The economic recession has resulted in a greater proportion of jobs being part-time and low-paid anyway. But when there is internal family pressure to maximize total income by having two earners, women will tend to take any job they can get, which by definition usually means a low-paid job with few prospects and little to offer by way of personal fulfilment. Even well–qualified women working in professions where, in theory, there is equality of opportunity, still regularly find themselves paid less than men because the structures of those professions do not facilitate promotion for anyone who is not able to give 100% of their time and energy to the job. That tends to exclude most women with children, because the reality for them is that family stability can depend on a woman being prepared to give up or in some way modify her personal ambitions in terms of career prospects. Even employers who claim to be enlightened and sympathetic by offering 'flexible' working hours usually do so only at the expense of promotions and career advancement. The fact that women take this in their stride by making 'invisible' modifications to their ambitions (by not going for extra training or refusing promotions and transfers) does not make the economic injustice any less real.

This familiar catch-22 situation is obviously related to wider issues within modern families. In practice most women make compromises of this sort without any direct coercion. But they rarely have any option to do otherwise, which is one reason why some (especially in top jobs) defer having children. This undoubtedly avoids the problem of an interrupted career, and in one sense is the obvious thing to do, because ultimately it is the presence of children which disrupts adult ambitions and lifestyles. It would make even more sense for women to choose not to have any children at all. But saying that merely highlights the nature of the difficulty, because almost any choice available to a woman is going to involve personal costs of a kind that men do not have to reckon with − whether by postponing the emotional satisfaction of having children for as long as ten or twenty years, facing the increased physical risks of having children at an older age, or indeed choosing not to have them at all.

This interconnected web of economic and emotional relationships is one of the major reasons why family breakdown is becoming increasingly messy and painful. In traditional families, women's role was clearly related to work in the home, as a result of which they became dependent and vulnerable. We are right to regret that, but we are deluding ourselves if we think anything substantial has changed. In the new situation women are doubly vulnerable, because now men are less disposed to accept mutual accountability because they think women are, or should be, financially independent. As a result of convincing ourselves that reality matches theory, and that women can in fact easily be self-sufficient, most female single-parent families find themselves poor and with little sympathy from men who tell them when relationships fail, 'You wanted to be independent in marriage, and you can't change the rules now just because things didn't work out.'

'A Shoulder to Cry On'

Women have always been expected to bear the emotional pressures of family life, providing a warm, secure, loving home environment for husband and children and being available to meet their wide-ranging emotional needs. In the light of changing social expectations, it has become fashionable to talk of men needing to develop their 'feminine' side, which is usually defined in terms of intuition, sensitivity, personal openness, and generally having a gentle image as distinct from the traditional macho image attributed to men. Whether these differences are absolute, in the sense of having some physiological gender basis, or relative in the sense of being the products of socialization, need not concern us here. Either way, they highlight yet another example of double standards on the part of society at large. For while 'feminine' characteristics are, in this context, seen as a good thing, traditional psychology still generally regards the female characteristics as inadequate, and the male ones as normal or healthy.

There is no shortage of evidence showing the impact of these attitudes. A mother's personal needs are often sacrificed for the good of the entire family. Not only that, but she is regularly blamed for the dysfunctional behaviour of others, such as violence on the part of a husband or the delinquent and anti-social behaviour of her children. It is a well documented fact that the incidence of depression and phobias of all kinds is much greater among married women than single women or men, and their consumption of tranquillizers is correspondingly greater. In the light of our previous analysis of the changes in family life, this is hardly surprising, for most women still have a low level of control over a situation whose demands and pressures are increasing all the time. Moreover, men often have an unhelpful functional approach to the emotions, most obviously highlighted in their different attitudes to sex, which men regularly regard as the starting point for emotional intimacy, whereas women see it the other way round.

All that we have said so far applies in relationships that are outwardly stable. Breakdown and divorce bring even greater emotional struggles, though on balance they seem to be greater for men than for women, at least in the long term. That does not mean it is easy for women. Being a single parent usually means economic disadvantage for women, which in turn affects their relationships with children, and possible future partners. But a woman is also realistic about the alternatives, and knows that remarriage is unlikely to be the end of emotional pressures, because the same burdens are still there, only a second time round they might be expanded to include as many as three different sets of children as well as a new marriage relationship (not to mention elderly relatives and responsibilities to the wider family circle). In addition, all this will have to be worked out in the shadow of memories of past failures, and the almost certain knowledge that future failure will also be blamed on her. Men typically adopt a pragmatic, even utilitarian approach to relationships, content to see how things work out, whereas women always invest much more emotional capital even into relationships that seem to have no long-term future.[4]

To imagine that women have been set free from emotional bondage is to take a very unrealistic view. The fact is that at the emotional level women today struggle with infinitely more complex demands than previous generations, facing contradictions and tensions all along the way. The modern woman is to be her own person, independent and free — yet also at the beck and call of others. She is to work at a job to make her contribution to the family budget, but she is also to be responsible for maintaining the home. She is to be free to choose whatever will bring her personal fulfilment, but her choices are constantly circumscribed by the duties of being wife and mother. She is to be independent, but always there when others need her. There is just one thing that distinguishes her from her grandmother: she has a choice to leave relationships that are destroying her. In theory, of course. For in trying to exercise this choice, increasing numbers of women find themselves subjected to physical and sexual violence which then emotionally damages them even further.

Violence

There has been a general rise in awareness of violence against women in recent years. Even now we cannot be sure that we know the full extent of it, because what happens in the home is still the most secret of all areas in modern life, especially when it concerns relations in marriage or other forms of partnership. By definition there are rarely, or never, witnesses to testify to what has taken place, and even when violence against women clearly occurs it is often not taken very seriously. In spite of much public debate, the authorities and society at large still generally assume that for a woman to be raped or beaten by a man she knows – particularly one she loves – is less serious than to be assaulted by a stranger, and in just about all cases there is a tendency, one way or another, to blame the woman for what happens. As well as domestic violence, there has also been an increase in all forms of harassment of women in the workplace, through physical, verbal, visual and other means.

Violence is rooted in the need to control other people.[5] It is a way of punishing those who break accepted norms of power and privilege, and society finds it easy to accept this in relation to racial or political violence. Political leaders justify acts of war by reference to the need to 'punish' or 'teach a lesson' to those who step out of line of the international consensus. It seems only logical to set violence against women within the same frame of reference. Yet many people are resistant to this, and instead of enquiring about the social structures and attitudes which provoke violence against women they prefer to understand violent men as individuals who are deranged or need help in some way. All the available evidence, however, shows that rape and violence are not so much about sex or personal gratification as about control and domination. At least one consequence of violence against women is to make them more afraid, and therefore more controlled and restricted in what they can do and where they can go. For example, statistically a woman who is alone in a city street is significantly less likely to be violently assaulted than a man in the same circumstances. But the perception of most women is the exact opposite and they, not men, are the ones who stay indoors out of fear. Similarly, women who are beaten by their husbands often keep silent because of their fear of them and the public shame that would result from being open about what is really happening.

We will return to violence again in a later chapter, because it is a major factor in family dysfunction. Here, we shall simply note some of its causes and consequences. Violence always has a cause, but the same immediate cause may not necessarily lead to violence in every case. People who try to resolve conflict through violence have usually learned it from their own formative experiences in violent families. Men beating their wives is not a new thing, though quite possibly the extent of it, and the reasons for it, may be different now than they once were. In old movies violent men were regularly the heroes, and they beat their women for a variety of reasons: when they defied patriarchal authority, or when their husbands were drunk or angry about something else, or when their husbands' meals were not to their liking, or whatever. Abusive words qualify as 'violence', just as much as physical assault. Indeed, violent men often use psychological and physical violence alternately, to keep their victims in suspense not knowing what might happen next, and thereby undermining whatever vestiges of security and self-esteem they have left.

Middle-class professional people tend to report domestic violence less than other groups. But that probably means they are better at covering it up. There is certainly no reason to suppose that 'Christian' families are immune. There is no one simple cause of violence against women. Patriarchy is certainly one element, though not the only one. Given the existence of other factors, however, it does provide a social framework within which violence can occur and appear to be 'justified'. Anything that challenges a man's dominance can easily become a catalyst for violence. Within the Christian world, some theologies have a tendency to encourage this thinking, even if they do not overtly approve of personal violence as a means of enforcement. Obviously this is not the only contributing factor to domestic violence, but it is often present. In terms of the wider culture, there is also evidence of a link between economic stress in men and violence against women, suggesting that the perceived loss of control in one area of life may lead to a need for greater control to be expressed somewhere else, and the home is the obvious (and easiest) place for insecure men to assert this.

So far as women victims are concerned, the long-term effects of violence can be totally destructive. They include a severe loss of self-esteem, self-hatred, withdrawal from contacts outside the home, drug and alcohol abuse and, eventually, disintegration of the personality (the ultimate submission). Short-term effects are physical injuries, or even death. Many women are murdered when they try to exercise their right to leave a relationship (though in such cases moving to end the relationship is more often an effect of previous violence, rather than its first cause).

Men

On the face of it, men seem to have generally survived pretty well in the upheaval of the family. Yet they face their own set of challenges at a variety of different levels.

Most men have a real problem with relationships, and have little idea how to deal with women. They love them, yet they are afraid of making wholehearted and open-ended commitments to emotional intimacy. They are dependent on women, but they fiercely oppose any notion of mutual accountability. They desperately long for women to approve of them, but they find it well-nigh impossible to ask for acceptance. They want – sometimes, expect – women to be there when they need them, but only to deal with immediate (and sometimes trivial) needs, rather than entering into open relationships. If they are honest, most men will recognize themselves here.

The most widely-held explanation for this state of affairs directly impinges on the nature of family life. Most researchers see men's uneasiness with themselves as the result of their own mother-dependent childhood, and the lack of a helpful male role model especially during their formative years. As boys grow up, this often leads to a love-hate relationship with their mother. On the one hand, she has great power over them, but on the other she is unable to do everything, and in a patriarchal context may be prevented from doing all the most important things. For many males, their first step toward personal autonomy occurs when they challenge the authority of their mother. It is only a small step from that for men to make a habit of defining themselves and establishing their own identity by rejecting and being 'set free' from women. Unless men have specific opportunities to work through these attitudes, the scene is set for a lifelong love-hate attitude to women in general. For boys who are raised in families where the father is rarely involved in matters relating to the home and domestic life, the image can be very powerful: to be a man is to be 'free' from women, and being a real man must involve psychological superiority over women, and the need to be dominant in all male-female relationships.

For these and other wider cultural reasons, the role models commonly available to men mostly define them by reference to such values as independence, power, and aggression. Maleness becomes identified with the need to have power and control in all areas of life. In spite of some changes, the world of work still operates on these principles. They are damaging in any context, but when they are applied to the family they can only serve to destroy any possibility of intimacy and openness in relationships. Needless to say, these understandings of what it means to be a man are also profoundly unChristian.

Men and Money

Paradoxically, even those men who might have subscribed to some of the values just described have not always been happy with their practical consequences. It has been aptly observed that while many women felt oppressed *within* the traditional patriarchal family, many men felt oppressed *by* it, and particularly by the burden of having to be the sole economic provider. In past generations a man was judged by his ability to feed, clothe and house his family. His main ambition had to be to rise as high as possible in the employment market to ensure that his family's standard of living would be as secure as he could make it. He threw himself wholeheartedly into the rat race of paid employment, and no matter what the discouragements he stuck with it, courageously doing the best he could for the sake of his family. When, inevitably, he was less successful than others, then he knew he could go back to the family for psychological respite. In the home, he would always have a special position and privilege. To his family, he was the best man in the world, and even when he lost out to competitors in the real world of work, he could still wield great power in the home.

Many writers describe the old patriarchal family as if it made life very easy for men, at the expense of women. It is nearer the truth to say that it often dehumanized both of them. In the case of men, it defined their role purely in economic terms, and gave them a distinctive personal identity only by reference to work. This is an insidiously destructive understanding of human nature, and many men still find that the loss of a work-defined identity leads to personal disintegration, whether through loss of work or retirement. Have you noticed how men always feel a need to define themselves by reference to their jobs? That is a long way from the Christian understanding of the worth of men and women, all of whom are made 'in the image of God'. It will be a long, hard slog, but we need to take seriously the challenge of enabling men to feel happy with defining themselves as husbands and fathers.

Despite all that, one might argue that the fixed boundaries of the traditional industrial nuclear family at least offered men some sense of 'security', in that everyone knew where the boundaries were, and who was responsible for what. Today, many men feel that the changing shape of the family has removed from them even that limited sense of their own worth. Generally speaking, it is no longer possible for a man to be the sole economic provider for a family, certainly not without taking on spare-time work in order to do so (though some men will choose this option to their own detriment sooner than accept the inevitability of economic partnership with a spouse). In any case, even if a man manages to provide for his family single-handedly to his own satisfaction, he is likely to find himself disapproved of by society at large as a person who has stuck with the old ways of doing things. If he manages to handle that, he is still likely to find himself disadvantaged by tax regulations in most Western countries. With the exception of people with inherited wealth or other forms of private income, the kind of traditional family in which it is financially possible for men to be the sole economic providers will disappear entirely in the course of the next decade or so. As this happens, even those men who think of themselves as progressive will find themselves forced to make some more or less painful adjustments to their self-image.

The economic realities of life for men in situations of family breakdown are also challenging, and largely parallel those faced by single mothers in the same circumstances, though as has already been indicated, men hardly ever find themselves in such desperate poverty as women.

Men and Their Feelings

We are facing a major crisis today in how to define what it means to be a man, and much of this centres around emotional issues. As men come to terms with the changing face of family values and structures, they are having to handle levels of emotional stress which would have been unthinkable for their fathers and grandfathers. The collapse of the traditional male role is threatening enough by itself, but that pales into insignificance when compared with the challenge of coming to terms with new ways of being a man. For if the 'new man' is to function as an effective partner in the modern family, he will need to be a good deal more emotionally open than any of his ancestors have managed to be. Nor is he likely to get too much assistance from women, who from a man's point of view can still seem unhelpfully ambivalent. On the one hand, they still seem to want men to be tough and strong (their old role), but on the other they are also demanding that they be intimate and open about their feelings.

What, then, does it mean to be a man? This is a much larger issue than many people appreciate. After a quarter of a century of the women's movement, at least we all know what the possibilities might be for women, even if not every woman is yet able to exploit them all.[6] But men are just at the start of this personal search for a new identity, and they have very little to guide them apart from groups offering wilderness retreats, and the kind of spirituality reflected in Robert Bly's best-selling book *Iron John*.[7] There is a major opportunity for the Church here.

Apart from such basic questions about personal identity, even men who accept that things have changed can still be threatened by the everyday reality of increased female competition in the workplace, and their wives' understandable expectations that they should take responsibility for some of the work in the home. Men who still wish to be 'traditional' face the same realities, and find it even harder to cope with them, particularly if they become personal issues and their own wives insist on going to work outside the home.

For generations, men's psychological well-being has been inextricably bound up with their expectations of marriage and the family. It is well known that men do not have the same open relationships with other men as women do among themselves. This is a result of the way the workplace has been structured. When competition is the basis of career advancement, it stands to reason that you would never want to expose your weaknesses to those whose main purpose in life is to take advantage of you. Consequently, the only place where most men could ever open up – to however limited an extent – was in the safety and security of the home, especially in the days when women took it for granted that their job was to give their men whatever they wanted, with no questions asked. We have already noticed how women were oppressed and exploited by this situation. But the other side of the coin is that men actually needed the family and marriage for their essential security. Statistics over a long period show for example that, on average, married men live longer than single ones, and are less likely to be criminal or to commit suicide. This is why divorce and breakdown come as a great shock to many men. A man can really love his wife, but be so insensitive that he literally has no idea how she really feels, and that she is about to leave him. That kind of man can suffer a profound loss of purpose and personal value from which he may never recover. Not all men suffer that way, of course, and there are others for whom breakdown is more about the disruption of lifestyle and their loss of public image than about the loss of a particular family. They can move on to new relationships more easily.

This is the context in which we need to place the rising incidence of domestic violence by men against women. It should go without saying that there is never any excuse or ultimate justification for violence. But those who are involved in ministering to men in this situation will do so more effectively if they understand as much as possible about some of its underlying causes. There has always been male violence against women. In the past it has even been admired as a part of the macho image men were supposed to project. The changing structure of the family, and especially any kind of breakdown in relationships, can only add to the pressures with which traditional men are now struggling. Though it is impossible to quantify, most researchers have a strong feeling that violence against women is on the increase, and that part of the reason is in some way related to men's feelings of frustration, failure and insecurity in the new situation. Men who find it difficult to cope can find an easy outlet for their anger by inflicting pain on women and children, hence the rising incidence of abuse in the home, and harassment in the workplace. Women become scapegoats for men's own insecurities. If a man fails to win promotion in work, he can blame the female competition, or female managers. If his marriage breaks up, he takes it for granted that it must be his wife's fault. By gradual increments, men can cast themselves in the role of helpless victims, and thereby justify (at least to their own satisfaction) victimizing others. Several Western countries have seen this on an organized level, with the rise of so-called 'fathers' rights' groups, who are trying to flex their muscles by, for example, going to court to get injunctions preventing their partners from having abortions, or from moving away with their children to start a new life in another city, or by campaigning for what they call 'equal' treatment of women and men in divorce settlements (which almost always means worse treatment for women).

Different men deal with these pressures in different ways, depending on their personality, temperament, and the nature of their family relationships. Men in traditional marriages are likely to have the most conflicts. They face the economic pressure of being solely responsible for adequate financial provision for their families, combined with what they are likely to regard as unfair and disagreeable competition from women in the workplace. If their wives share their traditional views, they may be able to mitigate some of this, but if not the pressures can become overwhelming – and one of the features of changing divorce patterns is the increasing number of people who separate later in life after marriages that can have lasted for twenty or even thirty years.

Danger – Men at Work

In discussing the problems facing women in the family, we have already given considerable attention to the conflict between work and home. Men also face many of the same demands, even if they experience them slightly differently. Men who try to be good parents and partners do not always find it easy to balance the quality of their home life against the insistent work pressure to go for promotions and to improve their position in the workplace. Promotion can often involve the need to move home to some distant area, which can be unsettling for children. Or it might require a man to commute for several hours a day, with the attendant reduction in the hours available to him to be with his family. This is a problem for many men already, and in large cities it is not uncommon for fathers of young children to be leaving home before their children are out of bed in the morning, and not returning in the evening until long after they have gone to bed again. This obviously increases stress for any man who takes his parenting responsibilities seriously. It also makes weekends and holiday times especially valuable – something that churches need to recognize in the ways they organize their activities. Despite many changes, men still find the world of work is at odds with their responsibilities in the home. Their jobs are organized and defined as if their family did not exist, and whenever they allow family responsibilities to impinge on work, by leaving early or missing meetings, they are likely to get more negative reactions than women would in the same circumstances. Men can easily find themselves in a no-win situation: they know their families need them, but the opinion of their work colleagues (at least on an official level) is that the job should always come first. Any man who refuses to comply is regarded as a wimp who is likely to lose out on the promotion ladder. It can be hard to live with conflicts of that sort, and wrestling with them in the midst of all the other challenges of the modern family is never going to be straightforward.

When men are also coping with the aftermath of separation and divorce, the same problems are magnified many times over. Single-parent families headed by fathers can have acute problems simply because it is impossible to be in two places at once, though single fathers have medium-term advantages over against single mothers, because they tend to have higher incomes and they generally stay single for shorter periods of time. But for the period when they are single parents, men probably face more social isolation than women. The fact that the role of the single male parent is not always socially acceptable means they typically have fewer networks for emotional support than women in the same situation.

Two things clearly emerge from this survey of the respective problems of women and men in the modern family. First is that there are no easy solutions, and we will not find the answers by looking to the experiences of the past. We are making families today with no role models, and that can be scary. When it works out well it can also, of course, be exciting and rewarding.

The second thing is that neither women nor men will be able to redefine the family single-handedly. We will need to learn to work in partnership, which in turn requires openness and a willingness to be in constant negotiation over family roles and responsibilities. Maybe our respective responsibilities will change at different stages of the family's life cycle. But co-operation and genuine sharing will be the only things that will enable us to create the new community for which we are all looking. As an ideal, that accords well with some distinctive Christian values, and modelling that may well be the most useful thing that the Church can do for today's parents.

5

BIBLE FAMILIES

It is natural for Christians to turn to the Bible for guidance on family life, as on other significant matters of faith. But for many people the Bible, far from providing an answer to their questions, is itself a part of the problem. Given the enormous social and cultural differences between Bible times and our own, how can we use the Bible in a way that will inform and empower our own family relationships so as to reflect the abiding values of the Gospel? How can we sort out what is still relevant, and what we may need to discard? For those who struggle with Christian faith in today's family, that is far from being a purely academic question. On the contrary, the answers they find can – and do – make or break family relationships. By way of introducing some of the pressure points, we will begin with a story. As it happens, what we describe did actually happen to a couple we know. But, give or take a few details, many Christian couples find themselves struggling with the same dilemma.

The Struggle for Relevance

Clare and Martin (not their real names) were a young Christian couple in their twenties. When they fell in love and decided to marry, the only thing that motivated them was their shared desire to be truly happy together, and for their new home to be a place where Christ would be honoured and served. Neither of them had given a great deal of thought to what marriage might involve, nor had they ever heard much about the subject in the context of regular Sunday worship. But as soon as they announced their intention, they discovered that, while their church was not the sort which would hold workshops or seminars on relationships, there were many quite specific, if unspoken, expectations about the way Christian partners ought to relate to each other in marriage. Clare and Martin had imagined that working out how their faith might be reflected in their relationship would be an essentially pragmatic exercise. Instead, they were amazed to find themselves sucked into a theological whirlpool in which they were soon out of their depth.

As she spoke with other women in the church, Clare discovered that being a Christian wife should involve her in being submissive to her husband. As a modern young woman, she was initially surprised by such talk, but the more people she spoke to, the more it was made clear to her that this was the Bible pattern for marriage. Since she wanted to be faithful to Christ, as well as being a good partner for her husband, she conceded that, while it might be culturally unpopular, it would be the Christian way for her to allow Martin to take the lead in all the major decisions affecting their new life. It took her some time to work through it all for herself, and eventually she felt happy enough with a submissive role to raise the matter with him. She was taken aback, and initially hurt, by his response. Far from welcoming her ready compliance to the Christian ideal, he was absolutely horrified at what she was saying. He had actually come across some of the same ideas many years before, because unlike Clare he had been brought up in the church. But he had always secretly hoped that he would never seriously need to wrestle with these notions in any practical sense. To him, any talk of submission was the denial of everything that he was hoping for from his relationship to Clare. To be honest, it scared him as well. The truth was that he had literally no idea what it might mean for Clare to be 'submissive' to him, nor did he have any inclination to find out. He could see no reason at all why they should not be good friends and equal partners in this new stage of their relationship. After all, they had fallen in love as two independent and equal persons, so what was to stop them building on that? The idea that he either could or should somehow be in control of his wife made no sense at all. 'If this is what Christian marriage is about', he mused, 'then you can keep it.'

But they did truly love each other, and so instead of backing out Clare and Martin determined to work through these conflicting opinions. Fortunately, they were in contact with a minister from outside their own church, who was a great source of strength to them both. By the time of their wedding day, they had resolved it all to their own satisfaction. They took a long, hard look at various Bible passages where submission was mentioned, and decided it was not for them. But when they came to exchange their vows, the presiding minister (who had not been party to their discussions) read this passage of scripture: 'Wives submit to your husbands as to the Lord. For a husband has authority over his wife . . . And so wives must submit completely to their husbands . . .' (Ephesians 5:22-24). Should they laugh or cry? Having been through it all in advance, they laughed – and got on with the business of working out their own understanding of what a Christian family should be.

Others would not be able to smile so easily. It is no laughing matter for the battered wife or the abused child to be given such advice. Frankly, if the submission of women to men is of the essence of the Christian family, then for many people it is going to make better sense not to be Christian. To be under the control of another person can never be good news for the oppressed and the wounded. Yet very many Christians struggle with precisely this issue as they try to work out how they are supposed to follow Christ within today's family. Moreover, much of the advice given by Christian leaders to the victims of violence and abuse reflects the opinion that the acceptance of male domination in marriage is the 'Christian' way to live.

This brings us to the very heart of what it means to be Christian and to be a responsible member of a family. It is a subject that many Christians find easier to avoid. But unless we deal honestly and openly with Bible passages that seem to promote the exploitation of women and children by men, we will have nothing to contribute to the renewal and healing of suffering families, whether our own or other people's. Women who find themselves trapped in violent and abusive relationships suffer extensive and destructive guilt as they try to rationalize what is happening to them by reference to the kind of theology which regards the submission of women to men as the essential foundation stone of a happy family. An unexpectedly high proportion of those who call for help from shelters for battered women begin to explain themselves by saying, 'I'm a Bible-believing Christian, but . . .'[1]

A Realistic View

It is understandable that at a time of rapid and unpredictable cultural change, we should all be looking for some markers that might guide us on our way and provide that sense of security which (probably inaccurately) we imagine our forebears enjoyed. Furthermore, it is natural and right that Christians should take seriously what the Bible has to say about family relationships, as on other matters affecting faith and lifestyle. But in this area, as in many others, using the Bible effectively is neither simple nor straightforward. It is very easy to be self-opinionated and self-righteous, and to develop a way of understanding whose main allegiance is not to the Bible at all, but to those social and political structures with which we ourselves feel most comfortable.[2]

We have already argued that the traditional Western industrial nuclear family is a practical family lifestyle only for a rapidly diminishing number of people today. We have also suggested that it is not in any sense an intrinsically Christian pattern. Like all other family styles through the ages, it is culturally conditioned. It is impossible to locate this kind of family in the Bible, and the insistence of some on doing so is not only having disastrous consequences for many Christian homes, it is also distorting our image of the way the Bible actually presents the family. Instead of asking how to turn the clock back to an age that has now gone for ever, we should be asking how we can live in the new circumstances in ways that will reflect the love of God and the values of Christ's Kingdom. But to free ourselves up for that, we will need to recognize that there is no single pattern for family life enshrined in Scripture, nor does the Bible contain timeless truths which are as valid for families today and in the future as they were for ancient Israel or the first Christian communities.

We have been reflecting together on this for the whole time we have ourselves been married (almost thirty years), and one of the few certain conclusions we have reached is that there really is no such thing as a Biblical blueprint for something called the 'Christian family'. No doubt that statement will leave us open to the accusation of promoting a watered-down faith that merely accommodates itself to the latest social trends. It is our contention, however, that we are doing exactly the opposite, for by going back to the teaching of Jesus in particular we are reverting to the very roots of the Christian Gospel. We are also, as we will seek to demonstrate shortly, placing ourselves squarely in the centre of the ongoing tradition of Christian history, and indeed of the Bible itself.

Christian Families

Christians have always accepted that families come in different shapes and sizes. Family dysfunction is nothing new, and has always characterized intimate human relationships. The idea that Christian families should expect to be free from problems is a recent phenomenon. Many of the great heroes of the past wrestled with the consequences of their own unhappy home lives. One of the most striking examples was John Wesley, who found it easy to leave home and embark on arduous mission work precisely because of his own dysfunctional family relationships. David Livingstone was another one who had an unhappy relationship with his wife. Indeed, his personal indifference to her needs and the problems she encountered in being, in effect, a single parent to their children, eventually caused her to lose her faith altogether.[3] Long before their time the apostle Paul may well have found himself in a similar situation.[4] In our own era, we all know of prominent tele-evangelists who have made a great show of believing in what they call 'family values', and even castigating other people because they do not match up to this standard – while at the same time themselves living in a completely different way.

We may regret some of this, but we cannot deny that it is all a regular part of life, even of Christian life. The 'Christian' family is no different from other families, and to try and pretend it is will do no good either for the Christian cause or for family life. One of the most consistent features of all our research for this book has been the repeated identification of prominent Christian leaders whose behaviour does not match up to their stated beliefs. Or, to express ourselves more carefully, their behaviour *does* match up to their beliefs, which begin with the assumption that the family is a hierarchy headed by men (responsible to God), under whom are women, children, pets and so on in descending order. The reality of life within many clergy families is that parents (almost always fathers) proclaim 'traditional family values' from the pulpit, while their own families are seriously dysfunctional, usually as a result of the violence and abuse that they themselves impose on their spouses and children. We must not exaggerate this of course, because thankfully not all Christian leaders live that way. But an empirical observation of the facts clearly indicates that the best we can say is that, within the Christian context (as elsewhere), the family has potential for great blessing, as well as for enormous harm and destruction. If, as some imply, the Bible's message is only about those families which match up to recent Western ideas of the industrial nuclear family, then we as Christians are in an unenviable position, with no distinctive insights of faith to contribute either to our own families or to those of others.

When we take the Bible seriously, however, and instead of ransacking it for proof texts look at the whole picture, we are presented with a rather different outlook. What immediately strikes the unbiased reader is not how different the Bible is from our experience, but how many points of contact there are. Wherever we look in its pages, we find exactly the same diversity of family styles as we encounter in everyday life. Notwithstanding their different cultural settings, Bible families were remarkably similar to our own, and shared many of the same struggles. Even the great heroes of the faith could be hard people to live with. Domestic violence, abuse of children, and exploitation of women are nothing new, even within the families of God's people.

Simply by reporting these unpalatable facts, the Bible emphasizes that God is concerned for all that goes on in family life. It also conveys some important insights into the way that faith can help make sense out of the muddle into which families so readily degenerate. It might seem unnecessary – even voyeuristic – to catalogue some of the problems encountered by Bible families. But it is worth doing, because when modern Christians turn to the Bible for guidance on family life, they often miss what is obvious. If we reduce the Bible to a collection of abstract ideals, it loses the ability to challenge and empower us to be the people God intends. But when we read its stories in the light of our own experience, we immediately discover that its world is not strange and alien: it is the same world of family conflict in which we still struggle to forge relationships that will bring growth and blessing into our own lives and those of others.

Bible Families

Families play a very important part in the Bible. Indeed, the entire Bible story is in effect a sequence of narratives about different families.[5] The realistic description of relationships in the very first family sets the scene for all that is to follow. As early as Genesis 3:16, Eve learns that 'your husband shall rule over you'. This is one of the first statements made in the Bible about human relationships, and it acknowledges a universal human reality: that women often find themselves put down and personally devalued even (or especially) by those men whom they love.[6] But this is not the only thing the book of Genesis says about relationships between women and men, nor is it the most significant comment. As a matter of fact, exploitation is listed as one of the consequences of the fall, and God's will as expounded on the first page of the Bible is quite different. There, the sexes are created equal: women and men are both 'in the image of God' (Genesis 1:27-8). Moreover, the possibility of them living together in an open and harmonious relationship is also underlined in the rather different story contained in the next chapter of Genesis (2:25). In Biblical terms, the structured hierarchies of the industrial nuclear family are not a reflection of the will of God. On the contrary, this is what happens when people reject the values of their creator.

From a theological point of view, what is wrong with patriarchal family models is that they are idolatrous. By creating a descending social hierarchy of God-Men-Women-Children, they also create a spiritual hierarchy in which women and children are denied direct access to God. Not only is this a contradiction of the creation stories of Genesis, it is also potentially an infringement of the first of the Ten Commandments. When men put themselves in the place of God they are denying not only the human rights of others in the family, they are also challenging fundamental aspects of the teaching of Scripture. Hierarchical dualism of this sort is not an authentic and intrinsic part of the Judeo-Christian tradition. The opposite is true: it is a sign that something has gone wrong. The first consequence of sin is a breakdown in relationships and the oppression of one person by another.

Bible families subsequently go from bad to worse. By the time we reach Genesis 4:1-16 fratricide is on the agenda, as Cain murders his brother Abel. Neither of these children experienced their family as a place of security. Cain had already suffered rejection within the family structure long before he lifted his hand against Abel. That scenario happens daily in modern families. There is no hatred so intense as that which can develop between family members.

A few pages further on, we come to the central family of the entire Old Testament. Abraham occupies a key role in the story of salvation history. When the Jews later confessed their faith, they did so in terms of their commitment to 'the God of Abraham, Isaac, and Jacob'. Moreover, Abraham is favourably mentioned as a great hero of the faith in the New Testament (Galatians 3:6-4:31, Hebrews 11:8-19). What kind of family did he have? Even a superficial answer to that question can hardly fail to highlight the fact that his was no 'ideal' family, and his own behaviour was the direct cause of its dysfunction. One way and another, every single person associated with Abraham suffered from his greed, lust, abuse, violence, and selfishness. The Bible hides none of the unpalatable facts as it describes how in turn he treated his wife Sarah as if she was a prostitute, encouraging the king of Egypt to have sex with her; how his insatiable sexual appetite led him into a relationship with another partner; and how he subsequently despised and rejected even his own children. The entire sequence of stories about him gives an honest picture of a man who misused his family for personal gratification, and then went on to despise those he had abused most seriously. Nor is this a unique case: examples of the same thing can easily be found in later Bible history (*eg* 2 Samuel 13:1-21). Many of today's families face the same problems.[7]

The Bible also documents the way family dysfunction is handed on from one generation to another. Given their own childhood experiences, Ishmael and Isaac were almost certain to find themselves entangled in unsatisfactory adult relationships. Isaac is the one whose story is recounted most fully. Since we all learn parenting skills from our own parents, it was entirely predictable that Isaac's family would disintegrate – and it did. Jacob cheated his brother Esau out of his inheritance (Genesis 27:1-45), and then in turn his sons went on to sell their brother Joseph into slavery (Genesis 37:1-36). At a later period, the same pattern of family dysfunction over several generations brought ruination to the royal houses of both Israel and Judah, with the cycle only broken when Joash was removed from his home and brought up by a foster parent in the ancient equivalent of being taken into care (2 Kings 8-12). The perpetuation of destructive cycles of family behaviour through many generations is not a modern phenomenon.

The family stories of other key characters present the same general picture. Think of Moses. By comparison with many other Bible people, we know very little about him in purely personal terms. One of the few things we do know is that he enjoyed a good fight with his brother Aaron and sister Miriam, even as an adult! Samuel is another key figure in the Old Testament story. Again, one of the few things we know of him in a personal sense is that he suffered the breakdown of his family life – this time, an enforced fostering in the name of religious devotion, as his parents abandoned him to be brought up by Eli, an old priest who had already made a mess of parenting his own sons (1 Samuel 1:19-27). The prophet Hosea experienced great anguish at the disintegration of his relationship with his wife. Ruth began with a happy and positive experience of home life until her husband died and she was left virtually penniless, only finding new meaning and purpose when she remarried and joined what today would be called a blended family. The New Testament presents a similar picture. Jesus told a story about a father with two sons. In spite of all the love that was showered on them, one almost destroyed himself with greed, and the other destroyed the family through pride. Inevitably, the father was frustrated (Luke 15:11-32). Jesus frequently met and affirmed women who had been abused and exploited by men. Even his relationship to his own family was not exactly idyllic (Mark 3:31-5).

This has been a random survey of life in Bible families. It is not exhaustive, but the sample is entirely representative and by making other choices we would not significantly have changed the general impression. Stories like this are obviously not intended as models for us to follow. If we understood them in that way, we would find ourselves seriously at odds with the central themes of Christian teaching. Anyone living next door to families behaving in this 'Biblical' way would be more likely to call the police or social service agencies than to admire them as families who are following the Christian way of life.

The problem is not with the Bible, but with the way we sometimes want to read and apply it. One of the Bible's great strengths (and a major reason why it is still worth reading at all) is its realistic honesty about the way human life is – and that includes its accounts of family life. The discovery that Bible families were just like ours must be good news – not because of the unsatisfactory nature of many of their relationships, but because in the midst of so much brutality, the Bible also provides us with a story of hope. Running through all its pages is the affirmation that, even in the worst kind of family malfunction, it is still worth trusting in God. Moreover, God can be trusted to take sides with those who are oppressed, abused and exploited. Faith is not a magic potion that dissolves the problems. Those, like Abraham, David and the rest, who make wrong choices are not let off, but have to live with the painful consequences of their wrongdoing. That is really good news for people who suffer, for the Bible's message is that God is with them in the midst of their pain – and on their side. Even if those nearest to them inflict injustice on them, God offers only unconditional love and acceptance.

This is not a book about interpreting the Bible, but it is worth emphasizing that Bible families are not presented as models for morality which Christians should imitate. Understood that way, they would be depressing in the extreme and would certainly raise serious questions about the viability of Christian faith. They are rather presented to us as mirrors, through whose reflections on life we can see ourselves more clearly. In the process, we can hear the good news, and be challenged about our own shortcomings, as well as being offered the possibility of new beginnings even for those who have been most deeply hurt. The Bible offers no quick-fix spiritual formula that will produce happy families.

Jesus in his Context

Family life in New Testament times was characterized by three major assumptions, with a long history behind them. First, family rights were essentially property rights. That is, families were patriarchal in the absolute sense that all the members of a household belonged to the dominant male. Even the Ten Commandments, which in some ways were ethically advanced and enlightened for their time, deal with adultery not as a moral or personal issue, but as a property issue. Having sex with another man's wife is placed in the same category as desiring 'his cattle, his donkeys, or anything else that he owns' (Exodus 20:17).

This meant, secondly, that women were always under the control and in the possession of men.[8] We have already briefly reviewed some aspects of relationships within Abraham's family. The basic assumption on which all his behaviour was founded was that women and children essentially exist for a man's benefit, to use as he likes. The reason Abraham's behaviour is not explicitly condemned in the Old Testament is because the whole story was handed on within the context of a patriarchal society in which that was the natural starting point. The way a man related to his family was not a moral issue. We see this especially clearly in relation to divorce, which was allowed for almost anything. The Old Testament placed virtually no restrictions on a man's rights to divorce his wife: 'Suppose a man enters into a marriage with a woman, but she does not please him because he finds something objectionable about her, and so he writes a certificate of divorce, puts it in her hand, and sends her out of his house; she then leaves his house and goes off to become another man's wife.' (Deuteronomy 24:1-2). Put that way, divorcing your wife sounds like selling a car when you get bored with its colour, or its performance begins to fall off – and of course, a woman had no rights at all to choose to divorce her husband, or whether to allow him to divorce her.

Thirdly, the positive function of a woman in this context was economic: she existed primarily for the purpose of producing children, who would support the family unit in the father's old age. A woman who did not reproduce was just like a car with an unsatisfactory performance. Some rabbis even doubted whether a woman who was unsuccessful at procreation would get into heaven.[9] The underlying philosophy of that has often been adopted in the Church, and is inevitably bad news for women, not to mention childless couples and singles.

It serves no useful purpose to criticize the Old Testament or Jewish heritage at this point. In all these respects it simply reflected the patriarchal values of its own times. In any case, by the time of Jesus questions were already being asked about some of these issues. Jesus' own teaching on divorce and remarriage to some extent reflected current debates that were taking place between the great rabbis of the day on the exact meaning of the term 'something objectionable' in the passage just quoted from Deuteronomy.[10]

In addition, though, Jesus challenged the accepted norms of his culture in some significant ways, not least by accepting women as partners with men in the spiritual quest. When Mary was criticized for talking about matters of faith instead of doing 'women's work' in the kitchen, Jesus specifically affirmed that she was doing 'the right thing' (Luke 10:42). He had a regular group of women who accompanied him and shared in his ministry (Luke 8:3), in striking contrast to other rabbis of the day, who generally regarded women as spiritually handicapped.[11]

Moreover, Jesus regularly identified himself with those who were the victims of exploitation arising in family contexts. Nowhere is this more clearly spelled out than in the story of a woman who had allegedly been caught in the act of committing adultery (John 8:1-11). The story does not reveal whether she had been formally tried and condemned in some way, nor does it indicate the precise nature of her wrongdoing (in a patriarchal culture, merely speaking to a man alone could be classed as 'adultery'). In any event, Jesus was invited to engage in physical violence against her by taking part in her execution. Such violence was not only condoned, but required by the Law. Jesus set it aside – and that was good news indeed for the woman, who discovered that 'whatever human law or custom may legitimate violence against women, it cannot stand face to face with the revelation of God's affirmation of all humanity'.[12]

Paul

Jesus' constant concern for outcasts of all kinds is so central to the gospels that no-one could plausibly question his commitment to belief in the essential equality of women and men, and of children and adults. But things are more complex with Paul. This is partly related to the nature of his writings, which were all letters, written in response to other letters or verbal communications, none of which now survive. With Paul we are always hearing only one side of a conversation, and that limitation should by itself warn us about the dangers of formulating hard and fast guidelines on the basis of what he writes. Nevertheless, some things are clear – and surprising, in view of the way he has been understood through much of

Christian history. In Galatians 3:28, Paul unequivocally affirms the equality of women and men, just as he asserts that there is no difference between slaves and free people, or between different races. Moreover, throughout his letters Paul mentions women whom he accepted as full partners in his own ministry, to at least one of whom he applies the title 'apostle' (Romans 16:7). And, in contrast to other teachers of the time, he argues that women have as much right to pray and prophesy in the public gatherings of the church as do men (1 Corinthians 11).[13]

At the same time, there are other statements which appear to say different things. The advice to families in Ephesians 5:21-33 is not the only significant passage in this regard, but we will focus on it here as it is the most relevant for our purpose. This is the widely-quoted advice already mentioned, about wives being submissive to their husbands. Several comments are in order. For a start, we need to place this in a broader context, and to note that it is a general code of conduct, widely accepted not only in early Christian circles but also in Judaism, and even some Greek circles as well. Paul was not the one who actually formulated these rules, and within the New Testament they are also quoted in Colossians 3:18ff and 1 Peter 3:1ff.

In addition, a close reading of the text shows this passage to be less problematic than we might imagine. It begins with the exhortation to 'Be subject to one another out of reverence for Christ' (Ephesians 5:21). This is the starting point for all our relationships as Christians, in the family as well as elsewhere. The Greek word translated 'be subject' (*hupotasso*) can also mean 'accommodate to' or 'give way to'. That is, Paul's readers are being encouraged to adopt flexible attitudes, and be ready to give way to each other. It is a bit like negotiating a 'stop' sign on a North American road. Everyone has the same right to go through the junction, and others have to respect that, but neither confrontation nor a free-for-all will be profitable, which is why everyone has to stop, and different people will have the right to go first in different circumstances. Paul expresses the same idea in Philippians 2:4, which is a useful commentary on this passage in Ephesians: 'Let each of you look not to your own interests, but to the interests of others'. It has been argued that the way Paul adapted what was a common code of social behaviour shows he was actually questioning the assumption of patriarchal domination, not reinforcing it.[14] Understood this way, the statement is about the mutual responsibility of husbands and wives, and Paul is saying that there are times in a relationship when a man should give way to his wife and recognize her interests as well as his own, while on other occasions the woman may need to do likewise. This is the same advice Paul gave in 1 Corinthians 7 when he wrote about matters relating to sex, divorce and remarriage.

At the end of the day, Paul may turn out to be more sensitive about relationships than we had expected, though still not quite as liberal as twentieth-century readers might wish.[15] He is certainly more progressive than 1 Peter, where a similar list of household duties leaves no doubt that a wife was expected to offer unquestioning obedience to her husband, and Sarah's tolerance of Abraham's violence is even held up as a model to be followed (1 Peter 3:6).

From Text to Practical Theology

In terms of practical theology, the key thing in understanding any text is not always what the text actually says, but what people perceive it to be saying, and it would be pointless to try to deny that many Christians see these Bible passages as somehow justifying the kind of behaviour highlighted in so many dysfunctional families elsewhere in the Bible. This is not arcane speculation about ancient texts and history. At a time when many Christian books on the family are arguing that submission by a woman to a man is the key to a happy marriage, and inflicting violence on children (euphemistically disguised as 'discipline') is the key to their personal maturity and ultimate happiness, it is a matter of immediate practical concern within the Christian community. The reality is that violence occurs widely in church homes, while ministers regularly advise the victims of domestic violence (if they believe them) to 'Stick with your partner', 'Forgive', 'Turn the other cheek' and so on. James and Phyllis Alsdurf are conservative Christians who want to take the Bible seriously, but writing in *Christianity Today* they had no hesitation in identifying this way of interpreting it as a major practical problem. It was a sobering discovery for them to realize that 'Over two-thirds of the women with whom we have talked stated that they felt it was their Christian responsibility to endure their husband's violence, and that in so doing they would be expressing a commitment both to God and to their husbands. Fifty-five per cent noted that their husbands had said that if they would be more submissive, the violence would stop; and one-third of the women believed that their submissiveness could be the key to stopping the violence.'[16] Our own research has shown that many Christian men somehow feel Biblically justified in beating their partners and abusing their children so as to give expression to what they perversely imagine to be some God-given order of hierarchical priority in the family.

In the light of the experience of many women and children, it is now time for us to be more radical about the terminology of submission associated with Bible passages like those highlighted. It may well be that an accurate exegesis will show that Paul is not always saying what he seems to be saying. But that is exactly the problem. To most ordinary people, what a Bible passage seems to say is what it must mean, and no amount of fancy theological footwork is going to convince them otherwise. To them, this just smacks of hypocrisy as if Christians want to have it both ways. Frankly, we are not doing the Gospel a service by going down that road. If there is a danger of misunderstanding, or if social circumstances have moved on from New Testament times, we must take these things into account.

In reality, even the most conservative Christians have already done that with other parts of Paul's advice. Take, for example, what is said about slavery in Ephesians 6:5-9. While the mutual accountability of slaves and masters might well have been an improvement over the prevailing first-century morality, everyone recognizes that in an absolute sense of right and wrong the application of wider scriptural principles makes any sort of master-slave relationship quite unacceptable. Though the seeds of slavery's destruction were always in the New Testament, it took the Church 1800 years to come to terms with it. Different social circumstances give us different opportunities to reflect on the Gospel's challenge to our own cultural norms, and the time has now come for us to accept that – whatever the Greek words may or may not really mean – submission is not a helpful concept for describing human relationships, no matter how carefully we try to define or redefine it.

To put it plainly, if as Jesus said the mere act of a man looking lustfully at a woman is adultery (Matthew 5:27-8), then holding the belief that a woman should submit to a man is the first step on the road to physical violence. The one is a logical development from the other. The idea that any person has rights over another is a dangerous and unChristian notion. It is the root cause of violence and abuse of all kinds. The same thing needs to be said in relation to children. It is easy to quote Scripture and encourage children to 'Honour your father and mother'. In essence, no-one would disagree that this is a noble ideal, though it needs to be balanced by the accountability of parents. But in today's social climate, Christians need to be aware of what they can be saying. Does it mean a child should obey her father no matter what he wants? This kind of teaching creates a climate in which exploitation and violence is not merely tolerated, but actually encouraged.

This is not the place to go further in the development of a Christian theology of the family. Indeed, the examination of texts is not the best way to do that in any case. For behind every theology there is a way of being Christian, and without spirituality there is no effective theology. We will only arrive at a theology of the family as we reflect on our actual experience of family, and of the ways in which we might minister both within and to the families of our own society. For this reason, if for no other, we can best progress this discussion by moving on to some very specific issues of practical ministry.

6

THE FAMILY AND THE CHURCH

In earlier chapters of this book we considered at length the challenges of being part of a family today. All families encounter stresses and strains as they wrestle with the everyday realities of living harmoniously with other people. Sometimes things go wrong, and disaster ensues. Families come apart, and individuals are deeply hurt in the process. This is often the point at which church leaders become involved. (Of course some of the families coming apart are those of church leaders themselves). Those of us who are involved in ministry with families need to appreciate that the provision of counselling in times of crisis – though essential – will not necessarily be the most effective way to help those families who are already in the Church, or to reach out to those who as yet are not. What families need from the Church more than anything else is the provision of an ongoing atmosphere of support that will assist in the positive development of wholesome relationships in the home, and the integration of matters of faith with the rest of life. When Christians say, 'We believe in the family', the only thing they often mean is that they are committed to preserving relationships that have fallen on hard times, and keeping families together regardless of the consequences. It is our opinion that if more energy was invested in the creation of positive attitudes towards relationships, we would help to create a more secure emotional future for ourselves and our children, as well as helping people to avoid some of the more obvious causes of breakdown in family life. If the Church does not take this need seriously, it can actually create dysfunction for those families associated with it. Before we can minister with integrity to families in times of crisis, we need to create churches that are themselves family-friendly.[1] In this chapter, we begin by taking a look at the one thing that all churches most obviously do: Sunday services.

Family-friendly Services

The one thing that families need more than anything else is support. Yet people wrestling with changing family circumstances can find it hard to identify the Church as an obvious source of such support. Many churches feel they have done all they can just so long as there are networks of pastoral care into which people with difficulties can be integrated. Personal relationships are important, but being a family-oriented church requires much more, and involves reappraisal of the actual structures of the church so as to take account of the needs of families.

Some time ago, John was in conversation with a man who at the time was in his mid-thirties. Like many men of that age, Donald (not his real name) was father to two young children. He wanted to be a good father, and had high aspirations for his family. He was determined that, unlike other men he knew, he would make his relationships with wife and children a major priority. Though he had a demanding job, he was prepared to make sacrifices at other points in his life, which meant weekends were set aside as a special time when the family could be nurtured and sustained. Donald was not a Christian, but he recognized the contribution that spiritual and moral values could make to the well-being of his family. He eventually reached a point where he felt it might be worth exploring what the Church had to offer, and so one Sunday morning (along with his family) he ventured into what for him was somewhat threatening and alien territory. Still, he knew the Christians in this particular parish were saying rather loudly that they believed in the family, and since he could identify with that, he thought it might be worth hearing what they had to say.

In spite of his own clearly articulated spiritual search, and his impression that the church shared his concerns for the family, it was not a good experience. So far as he was concerned the church might be prepared to *say* 'We believe in the family', but in reality its structures actually operated in ways that he felt undermined the integrity of his own family unit. For parents who were working all week, and who needed to maximize quality time at weekends, a central component of family nurture would obviously need to begin with both of them being physically present with their children. The realization that the church had a different agenda only began to dawn on him when, at the church door, his two-year-old was taken off into the creche by a stranger whom he had never met in his life before. Then his six-year-old was shunted into a Sunday School, again to be placed in the care of a total stranger. While Donald was working through a mental checklist of all the potentially damaging things that could happen to his children at the hands of these strangers, his wife was collared by other unknown, if well-meaning people, who tried to sign her up for groups and clubs that, they assured her, were especially – and exclusively – for women like her. They were certainly not open to men, anyway – and within a matter of minutes of his arrival in church, Donald found himself asking why he was there. He had committed himself wholeheartedly to spending time with his wife and children, as part of which he felt it was important that they engender some sense of values and spirituality – and had gone to church with a sense of expectancy and hope. Yet he found that what was for him the starting-point of good relationships – actually being with his family – was the one thing he was unable to do in the church. Needless to say, he never returned. He was too concerned about nurturing his family to impose on them what he perceived as the potentially damaging individualism which he had encountered at the church door. It was hard enough being apart from them all week, without volunteering for it on Sunday mornings. Donald's experience was not unique. It was not even unusual, and is being repeated in Western churches of all denominations every Sunday in the year. If we are serious about nurturing families, we will have to ask some hard questions about our structures. If our churches are not family-friendly, then why should we expect families to come to them?

Individuals and Community

Before exploring some things that will require attention, it is worth pointing out that we are not here advocating that churches should become child-centred. In the 1960s and 1970s a lot of British churches experimented with what they chose to call 'family worship'. More often than not, what they did on such occasions was not family worship at all: it was children's worship, at which adults happened to be present, and in the course of which were often made to feel uncomfortable by being invited to do childish things. Of course, that can sometimes be a salutary lesson for adults, because when that happens they are only getting a taste of the way children and teenagers regularly experience church, when they are expected to fit into services that are designed exclusively from an adult's point of view. But another problem with so-called 'family services' is that they have often been used to endorse the image of the industrial nuclear family as the only possible lifestyle, and as a consequence other people have felt excluded, especially childless couples and single people (who may or may not be parents).[2]

One of the major issues facing us today is the question of how to build meaningful communities. For two hundred years and more, the dominant philosophical ideology of the Western world has emphasized the importance of the individual. Whatever its faults, Marxist communism was the only coherent world-view to challenge that. But with its demise, the creed of the individual is now accepted by politicians and economists alike as the way to shape the world of the next century. When she was British prime minister, Margaret Thatcher once went so far as to assert that there is no such thing as community, only individuals. But in spite of all the political hype and the encouragements to be individually and personally responsible for ourselves and no-one else, the human spirit still recognizes this as a very impoverished way to live. People need other people. To be truly human, we need to belong somewhere, to be accepted and affirmed by others in relationships of openness and unconditional love. At one time, the family provided that, but this is no longer universally the case. A major reason why many younger people find relationships difficult is that they have no models to give direction. The models they have from their own upbringing are often flawed and unhelpful, and the last thing they want is to repeat the mistakes of their own parents. As a result, consumerism has hit the family market in a big way. It is now possible to go on courses to learn absolutely everything about relationships and parenting, as if harmonious families can be created in the same way as you might bake a cake or tune a car engine. Even marriage enrichment courses sometimes operate on this principle, assuming that if only you can find the right levers to pull and parts to adjust, a relationship will deliver whatever you need.

We have come to regard relationships (including especially those in the family) as a kind of business contract. This is evident from the increasing number of people who marry but who base their relationship not on commitment to one another, but on a separate document spelling out who will get what if and when they decide to break up. Everyone's ideal scenario is still the possibility of a couple being unconditionally committed to each other for life, but it can be difficult to envisage such a thing if your previous experience of family saw your own parental home disintegrate in violence and injustice. As a result, increasing numbers of people are planning for the worst while hoping for the best.[3]

The only way we will break out of this self-perpetuating cycle of defeat and despair is if we can find living examples of people of different dispositions and outlooks being together in harmony, working through their differences in a spirit of mutual respect and humility. The single most valuable thing the Church can do for families today is to model life in that sort of community. Openness, acceptance, the creation of safe spaces where we can be ourselves, sharing our weaknesses as well as our strengths – these are all hallmarks of the kingdom of God. Relationships are the all-important thing for families today, and Christians need to face the challenge of moving on from merely talking about them, to actually demonstrating them. People are searching for new ways to belong, and when the Church begins to model good practice in relationships, it will not only encourage and empower those families it already knows, but it will also find itself fulfilling the evangelistic mandate to share the good news more widely through the quality of human love (John 13:34-5).[4] The problem is that the life of Western churches (as distinct from churches in other parts of the world) tends to be centred on theology and abstract doctrinal propositions. But the Gospel is not about the transmission of religious information: it is about renewed lifestyles. Spirituality, not theology, was the central focus of Jesus' message. Being a disciple is the first act, and rationalizing about its meaning is the second. When we get things the wrong way round, it is hard to be a community.

Worship

It has been argued elsewhere that worship is central to the Church's life and witness, and what is true of Christian mission is no less true when it comes to nurturing families.[5] Experiences of authentic worship will both contain and communicate the whole Gospel for today's families. But what do we mean by worship? A phrase we have often used in workshops is that worship is 'all that we are, responding to all that God is'. When we consider 'all that we are', we can begin to see some ways in which our worship might address the needs of families.

It can be a very useful exercise to take that phrase, 'all that we are', and make a check-list of your own Sunday congregation. Better still, do it with the congregation, and allow them to describe who they think they are (which could easily be quite different from the opinions of clergy and other leaders). Then ask how what you do in worship meets the needs and reflects the spiritual concerns of that varied group of people. Repeat the exercise and extend the list by reflecting on the people in the wider community, and their needs. And keep doing it, because it is all too easy for worship to come to reflect the concerns of only a very narrow band of people. By acknowledging the richness of the human community, and actively creating a space for everyone, we can make a major contribution to the development of an experiential model for family life: the ability to love and be loved, in a warm, accepting and caring community of women, men and children.

In the Women, Religion and Violence project set up by the Network of Ecumenical Women in Scotland (NEWS), women who had been subjected to domestic violence were asked about their attitude to the Church. They identified several things that would need to change for them to feel a sense of identification with Christians. First came the observation that most churches have few women in leading positions. Second was the way that church people often dress, which they saw as different from their own style. Another major concern was the fact that victims of violence and abuse never hear themselves mentioned at any point in a typical service. Whenever families were mentioned in church, they said, they seemed to be ideal stereotypes, with children and parents who were too good to be true. They felt that while the poor and destitute of far-flung corners of the world might well be prayed for, those being abused in our own communities were usually ignored. Indeed, they had a strong impression that not only did the Church rarely condemn domestic violence and abuse, but implicitly seemed to encourage it by its own perpetuation of a patriarchal hierarchy, which sometimes gave more sympathy to the offender than to his victims.

We need to take such comments very seriously. For one thing, they reflect our own inadequate understanding of the breadth of Bible stories about families. We have already seen that the questions raised by these stories are the questions of modern families. Preachers and teachers need to take account of that. Instead of presenting only disinfected and idealized images of the Christian family, we should be helping people to engage in a Christian way with the families they already have. Remember that families suffering serious dysfunction are not only outside the Church: they are inside it. How can we minister effectively if these facts are ignored?

The striking thing about these observations is that none of them is theological or faith-centred in any profound way. Those abused women were not saying they found the Gospel irrelevant. Far from it: the breakdown of relationships often leads to an intensification of the spiritual search. The things they named were all structural. Without minimizing their importance, we might almost say they were cosmetic. It certainly would cost churches nothing to implement them. But when we find it so hard to create space in our worship for such simple things, is it surprising that people with these needs should feel alienated?

Think of another example, this time a personal one. At an earlier stage in our family life, John regularly visited different churches as a guest preacher, and Olive often accompanied him. At the time, our oldest son was just a toddler, and so while John would arrive reasonably early for a service and be ushered into the vestry to meet with the church leaders, Olive would take a longer time to wander around the area and would appear at the main door of the church only in time for the service to begin. Mostly, no-one knew who she was. To them she was the new single mother on the block – and they usually reacted accordingly. While industrial nuclear families were welcomed with warm smiles, and even openly recruited for the life of the church, she would be conscious of being ushered in as quickly as possible, with an absolute minimum of verbal formalities. That did not mean her arrival was unnoticed. Far from it, because the regular attenders at church were quite likely to ask questions among themselves, sometimes in loud whispers, in the perverse effort to find out who she might be, where she might live, and so on. They would never address these questions directly to her, of course. Then at the end of the service, things were totally different. As soon as she was known to be the preacher's wife, people who had been remote in their welcome and scurrilous in their gossip suddenly acted differently. Which reception most accurately reflected the life of those churches? The answer is obvious, and highlights a major challenge to our nurture of families.

Language

'The medium is the message', and it is not only what we do, but the words we use, that will have a profound effect on a church's accessibility to the family.

How do we describe the church itself? In recent years it has become fashionable to try to make the church user-friendly to families by describing the congregation as a family, maybe qualified by adding that it is 'the family of God'. It is an easy mistake to make, but one that is better avoided. For one thing, the family is not a major Biblical image of church, and so has no deep roots within our historical tradition. More significant, though, is the fact that while churches can model ways of living in community, relationships with people in the church are subject to different constraints from relationships in a family. There are different boundaries, especially in relation to physical intimacy, not only between fathers and mothers, but also between parents and children. There are also boundaries for appropriate physical contact in the home, and we shall refer to these in a later chapter. But it is nevertheless true that parents and children can make physical contact with one another in a way that would be improper between children and other adults. The way we describe the church needs to give clear signals to that effect. For children to be on first-name terms with adults in the church creates a safer atmosphere than the more old-fashioned tradition of regarding them as honorary 'aunts' and 'uncles'. In real-life families, uncles and aunts are the very people who often abuse children. It may be regrettable that it is necessary to safeguard our children in this way even in the church, but that is the reality, and the recognition of appropriate parameters expressed in suitable language is important. The Church is a community, not a family.

The language used in hymns is something else to be taken seriously. For women and children damaged by violent and abusive relationships, it is not good news to discover that so many hymns only seem to be about the spiritual experience of men. It is simply no longer part of the English language to write and sing about 'men' as if that means women and children as well, and to do so can only serve to reinforce the generally patriarchal image from which the Church already suffers in the eyes of many people. If the Church is only about men's concerns, and if your life has been blighted by men, why would you want to be a Christian? Christians in Britain (as distinct from North America and Australasia) have been far too slow to realize the importance of this issue of language, but the reality is that it can be a major stumbling block to the progress of the Gospel. If hymns are to be spiritually uplifting, then everyone needs to find themselves in there – especially those who have already been marginalized or excluded from the life of the community in other ways. Nor is this exclusively a problem found in older hymns: some of the very worst examples are to be found in popular British hymns written in the last twenty years.

But our language of God is perhaps the most important of all. This is not the place to engage in a detailed exegetical investigation of Christian words for God. But in terms of resourcing and supporting families at the practical level, it is not helpful to continue to use exclusively male language for God, especially when that is combined with patriarchal imagery. In essence, this is not a historical or theological issue, because Christians have always affirmed that God is beyond sex and gender, and the Bible itself uses a mixture of both male and female imagery to describe God. But for people wrestling with the changing shape of the family – and that includes those for whom things are working out, as well as those who struggle – male imagery is generally bad news. This applies especially to those who suffer from sexual abuse at the hands of their fathers, for whom the notion that God is a father (even a very perfect one) makes no sense at all, and is actually distorting a proper Christian understanding of who God is.

Preaching and Teaching

An American friend of ours spent a few years ministering in a British church. During that time, her church mounted many training courses, mostly related to mission and evangelism. She noticed that not many young people attended, and so persuaded the church to allow her to lay on a training course specifically for teenagers and young adults. The topic she chose was relationships. Some older people in the Church found it so predictable that they were doubtful about its usefulness. But her subsequent experience highlighted a major gap in the Church's preaching and teaching ministry. Though the kids who attended were all regularly involved in the life of the Church, at the very first meeting they told her they had no idea that Christians had anything distinctive to say on the topic of sex. The minister was amazed, and so were other members of the congregation. But at a time when they were making major decisions about personal lifestyle, none of these young people had picked up anything relevant from the Church. Once they were given the chance to talk about relationships, virtually none of them turned out to be actually opposed to a Christian understanding: they just had no idea that there was such a thing.

If that is true of a subject that historically has been a major concern of Christians through the ages, then how much more true would it be of other family issues today? How much guidance does the average church give people on matters relating to domestic violence or sexual abuse, not to mention the pressures of parenting and of forming new relationships in the context of blended families and the like? Most churches seem to have abandoned any effort to minister in this area, and these subjects are never mentioned in sermons except to condemn lifestyles that are deemed unacceptable. At the same time, some of the people who sit in our congregations struggle with these things, and because of the lack of Christian teaching on them they are forced to look for counselling and guidance from other sources. Some ministers no doubt deliberately avoid such subjects, because they know that their own families are not perfect models. But the sharing of our own burdens can help and inspire other people, and 'bearing one another's burdens' is one of the few things the New Testament quite specifically recommends us to do (Galatians 6:2).

While on the subject of preaching, it is worth reminding ourselves that the Gospel is good news. For those who are struggling to be the best they can at home, it is not good news to have guilt piled upon them. Ultimately, that means all of us, for even the families that seem most satisfactory have problem areas in their relationships. A relationship arises out of the interaction of two or more people in a particular context, and when things go wrong in the home, it seems to be natural to blame ourselves. The lack of self-esteem is a major problem in many domestic relationships, especially on the part of women and children. We have already mentioned the problems facing women who choose to invest time in raising their children, only to discover that they have become 'just a housewife'. When women are subjected to violence, and children are abused, whether physically through being beaten, or sexually, verbally, mentally, or whatever, the victims always have a tendency to blame themselves for what has happened – often encouraged by the abuser, who thereby thinks he is letting himself off the hook.

The Gospels are full of stories of how Jesus met with people in exactly these circumstances, and how he consistently lifted them up, and affirmed them as people of great value. For people with difficult home circumstances, to be repeatedly criticized in sermons, either directly or by inference, is not the Gospel. Theologically, we might say that sin is always involved in situations of dysfunction and breakdown, but sin is not always something that people do. It is often something that people suffer. They are, in the words of Chinese evangelist Raymond Fung, 'sinned-against'.⁶ To people like this, the good news does not say, 'You are responsible', but 'You can be responsible – and with Christ's help you can pull through'. More grace and less guilt will make for family-friendly experiences in our worship.

Changing Lifestyles

As we have already indicated in some of the earlier chapters, things are changing very fast in today's world. One of the few things we know for certain is that no-one really knows where we are headed, but wherever it is we will be going there in the fast-track. Some quite fundamental features of church life may need radical overhaul to meet the needs of the next century, including some hallowed traditions such as the times and nature of church activities.

Already, Sunday services at traditional times are becoming increasingly problematic even for those people who belong to the Church, not to mention those whom we might be wishing to reach. In terms of families, we might ask whether our services take place at the most helpful times of day. Churches in North America and Australia have generally managed to be more flexible, but the traditional times of British church services still suit the milking times of cows on medieval farms. Milking cows is not the same as feeding babies, however, and as a result church schedules are frequently at odds with the needs of small children and their parents. Nor do they make a lot of sense for families that have been through divorce, because Sunday is often the only day that the noncustodial parent has for spending time with her or (more usually) his children. When grandparents live at a distance, it is also often the only opportunity when a visit is practical. Even families that have not suffered major disruption or who do not need to visit grandparents are finding life busier and busier, and Sunday can be the only day to do the shopping.

Faced with the changing shape of the family, new forms of support mechanisms are emerging all the time in the wider culture. It is easy for the Church to be negative about some of them, especially when they involve different ways of spending Sundays. We need to learn from our own history the dangers of challenging and subverting indigenous family structures. Before the arrival of white settlers in Australia, aboriginal culture had a highly developed network of family support, which was then systematically dismantled by the imposition of Western values. As recently as the early 1960s, white state governments in Australia were sending raiding parties into aboriginal homelands to kidnap children and place them in urban foster homes, so they could be brought up in a 'civilized' fashion. Where this policy was 'successful', and aboriginal culture collapsed, it led to enormous social problems, notably alcoholism and homelessness – not to mention a huge legacy of guilt that now burdens many sections of the Australian population, particularly in the churches. The parallel with some church practices in Britain is obvious. When we insist on working against the cultural support networks – however problematic they might seem to be – trying to reach children by enticing them away from their own home and parental lifestyle, then we are sowing the seeds of tomorrow's problems, for both church and children.

Some years ago we were involved in ministry in a Chinese church which had an interesting way of addressing these questions. In their particular circumstances, they were trying to reach out to non-Christian families, as well as ministering to their own. Many were restaurant workers, which meant they were out of bed very late on Saturday nights. There was no point trying to have a Sunday morning service: no-one would come. But they did have a morning class for children, at which they taught Chinese language and culture. Then at about 3 o'clock, the parents of these children would come and join them and all ages together would have a time of worship. Next would be a community meal, which could take them through to 6 or 6.30, following which the young people would play table tennis (this being a game with particular appeal to Chinese people), or just sit around and chat and play music, while the adults would spend time in groups studying the Bible, or discussing other matters of mutual concern.

Growing churches in many countries are moving towards this kind of pattern of worship and community building. It matches modern lifestyles, and far from being some trendy new discovery, it also mirrors the way the earliest Christian communities met, as documented in the New Testament. The atmosphere of such a gathering creates a different dynamic for worship, and whenever food is involved there is always a place for everyone, regardless of their age or marital status, to be a part of the life of the community. The experience of base Christian communities all around the world is showing us that this kind of move forward that is also a rediscovery of our historical roots can be an important sign of the kingdom for today's world, calling people to follow Jesus as well as creating churches that will facilitate spiritual growth in families of many different shapes and structures.[7]

7

SUPPORTING PARENTS
AND CHILDREN

In the remaining chapters of this book we wish to pick up some of the issues that were highlighted earlier, and to give some general indicators as to how churches might provide positive support and nurture for people involved in different family circumstances. A word of caution is necessary, however, for what is relevant and useful in one context will not necessarily be appropriate somewhere else. There is a constant temptation in the Church to pick up a good idea that has worked for somebody else, and simply transplant it into another situation. That rarely works, because human needs are so diverse. Not only the needs, but also the acceptable ways of meeting them, will vary from one cultural context to another. What works well in a suburban middle-class church may not be relevant in a working-class or inner-city neighbourhood, and vice versa. Ministering to people must always begin and end with being sensitive to who they are, and that also means being realistic about who we are ourselves.

Some things, however, are not culturally relative. It is universally true that supporting and nurturing families is not the same thing as doing things for them. Church people love to do things for other people, whereas Jesus' model was one of working alongside people, and creating safe spaces where they could explore their own possibilities for themselves. This is the way we need to work with families. It is not a matter of prescribing what the ideal family should be like, nor of dictating the 'right' answer to every question. In relationships, there rarely is a single answer that will be right in some absolute sense for everyone. What we share in this chapter and the next is neither exhaustive nor prescriptive. We aim to sketch out some of the key needs experienced at different stages of family life, and to give some general indications of the kind of things that can be helpful. But think of them as a compass, giving a general sense of direction, rather than a detailed road map showing the precise route to take.

Everyone relates to a family at some stage of their life, and at different stages of life we relate in different ways. Family relationships are cyclical in nature, as we move from childhood to adolescence and through to adult life. Up to that point, we are always minor players in a family network that has been created by other people, usually parents, grandparents, and other relatives of their generation. As adults ourselves, we may choose to form our own relationships which then become the centre for the development of a new family, and lead in turn to the experiences of being parents and grandparents – or childless. We may also develop ongoing relationships with nieces and nephews, as well as our own brothers and sisters, or we may leave behind the wider family network to which we are biologically related, replacing it with other friendships that, in social terms, then become the equivalent of 'family'.

A circle has neither beginning nor end, and being part of a family gives a sense of belonging somewhere in the ongoing sweep of history – of being a significant link in the chain from one generation to another. We could therefore start to describe the cycle of family life from any number of points. In any case the various stages are all intertwined with one another, and it is impossible to keep them entirely separate. But for the sake of clarity we have chosen to begin in this chapter at the point where two adults become parents, and to tackle other parts of the cycle separately.

Becoming a Parent

Becoming a parent for the first time is one of the most exciting moments of a couple's life, as well as one of the most daunting. To be entirely responsible for the life of another person – especially one as vulnerable as a young baby – is an awesome responsibility. The first few weeks of being a parent are often filled with activity, as relatives and friends make the obligatory pilgrimage to admire the new arrival. Couples who live at some distance from their own parents might easily find themselves swamped by grandparents who are understandably pleased, but who ignore the realities of the situation and without invitation arrive to stay for extended periods of time, expecting the new parents to feed and entertain them at a time when they are already working hard just to cope with the baby. They may also be under financial pressure, and the last thing they need is the arrival of two more adults with the accompanying pressure on the domestic budget.

Grandparents can be both incredibly helpful and incredibly selfish at this time. The pressures are only increased when a large distance separates them from their newly born grandchild. All too often, new parents find their lives invaded for the first two or three weeks, and then they are left to fend entirely for themselves thereafter. This is also the point at which post-natal depression most often begins, and if that natural condition is combined with aggressive or insensitive grandparents it can take some time for the new parents to recover. Inevitably, it is likely to be the mother who bears the brunt of this pressure. She has already gone through pregnancy, brought the child to birth, and is likely to be losing sleep as the baby needs regular feeding – while fathers can give the appearance of sleeping all night, and then going off to work during the day to get away from it all.

New mothers are very vulnerable at this time. Knowing exactly how to support them, however, is not always easy, and is largely going to consist of being available and ready to offer whatever help may be welcomed. Enterprising churches will not wait until a baby is born to offer such support. We recently visited a church which had a regular group 'for bumps and bundles', which provided a space for pregnant women and those with small babies to meet together for mutual support and sharing. The few weeks immediately before a birth can be very special. For some women it will be their first experience of not being in full-time employment, and even if they are planning to return to paid work soon after the baby's arrival, it can still be disorienting. As with so many other aspects of family counselling, the help offered within a group of people with shared experiences is invaluable here, and can be a good way for people to make new friends, and to talk informally about matters of common concern. Loneliness is a major problem for many new mothers (as distinct from fathers), and anything the church can do to introduce them to others in the same situation is bound to be positive and helpful. It is amazing how many lifelong friendships are forged through contacts made in ante-natal classes. Remember also that any major life change usually raises questions of a religious or spiritual nature, and many women report that giving birth is a spiritual experience.[1]

Can I handle it?

Not every expectant mother wants to have a child. Despite the widespread availability of contraception, and the greater choices now available, people still end up having to make unenviable decisions. A few years ago, a close friend welcomed us home from an overseas trip with the news that she was pregnant. The problem was that for her at that moment, it was not good news. She already had several children, and her age raised questions about whether she would bear another healthy child. Inevitably, she was wondering if she should have an abortion – encouraged by her husband, who saw this as an easy way out of a situation with which he himself was unhappy. They were both keen Christians, and some of their friends had a simple answer to their question, believing that abortion must always be wrong.

When faced with matters that have been the subject of intense moral debate, and on which many Christians have strong opinions (on both sides), it will always be tempting to try and dictate answers to other people. But we can never make decisions on behalf of another family. We might think we know what we would do in the same circumstances, but unless we have ourselves been there it is impossible to be sure how we would react. For the wise counsellor wishing to help a family on a longer-term basis the priority will always be to help people gain access to the maximum information, so they can decide for themselves. Of course, it is never helpful to leave people floundering, and in this particular instance, we did encourage our friend not to make a decision through indecision. But it was not our business to be directive, and we were most help by being open and listening and praying through individual aspects of her situation. It soon emerged that her uncertainty about pregnancy was just one expression of doubts about other relationships, particularly with her husband. Had we tried to move her in one particular direction, then regardless of which direction that was, the space for further personal growth would have been closed off. As it was, she made her own decision and through that a family which was near breaking point has subsequently grown and been strengthened.

'Can you "do" my baby?'

Much ink has been spilled arguing about whether the Church should baptize the children of parents who are not themselves members. It would be an unprofitable distraction to engage with that debate here. But in terms of practical care, this kind of request needs to be seen in the context of the Church's mission. It is one of those classic instances where the Church can seem to be hypocritical – proclaiming its belief in the family, but unwilling to welcome parents and their children as fully into the life of the Church as they wish to be. For people who are unchurched, actually breaking into the alien environment of church culture to request baptism for their child takes such an enormous effort that doing so is in itself often a significant statement about their own spiritual search. When people come knocking at the church door of their own volition, this is not the point at which to turn them away, and certainly not on the basis of a theological argument that will mean nothing to them, and may only serve to reinforce the impression that church is an unreceptive and threatening place for ordinary people. Bishop John Finney correctly observes that 'Whatever the theological implications the evidence suggests that in practice parents need to be shown total welcome and also a way in which they can find out more about God in their own time.'²

Lay people can provide the most user-friendly line of communication with new parents at this point. If, as we believe, a key provision for family ministries is a parenting group, then members of such a group are likely to be ideally placed to share their own experiences – of faith as well as family – at such a time, and to offer friendship and support in a relevant way. Many denominations have produced good resources for use with parents enquiring about baptism, including videos which can be left with a family to watch and discuss at their own convenience. But in our experience, one of the most valuable things you can do with a family is to pray. Strangely, this is one of the things that Western clergy (especially men) find very hard to do in anything other than a self-conscious way. Yet prayer is the starting point of a spiritual journey for so many who are coming to faith today. Nurture of a family does not need to begin in the church building, and it can be some considerable time before they feel easy in coming to a service. Some may never make it, for all the reasons discussed in a previous chapter. No doubt different churches will reach different conclusions about baptizing infants (not to mention those that reserve baptism only for adult believers). But no one can afford to turn people away at their point of felt need, and then return to their homes five or six years later to invite their child to join activities such as Sunday Schools. Those who do might get the response they deserve.

Parents and Toddlers

As babies grow into toddlers they need the company of other children in order to develop their own personalities. Groups are not just for the benefit of parents: with the shrinking size of the family, they also play an increasingly important role in the socialization of our children.

It is worth spelling out a few definitions here. Parent and toddler groups are exactly what the name suggests: parent and child are there together all the time. While all the adults and all the children present obviously interact with each other, no adult takes responsibility for the overall care of someone else's child. It is important to differentiate between parent and toddler groups and nursery care. Though requirements vary from one country to another, under most Western legislation the laws that govern the two sorts of provision are quite different, and once children are being left in the care of another person there are statutory requirements to be fulfilled. A creche is therefore a different entity from a parent and toddler group.

We have noted in a previous chapter the urgent and increasing need for good quality child care while parents are at work, and some churches may well find they have suitable premises that could be used for this purpose. With the employment of properly qualified staff this is one area to which far-sighted churches should be giving some attention. Key considerations for churches thinking of this are quality (it needs to be an enriching experience for children) and accessibility (it should not be too expensive), as well as the need to remember not to exclude non-working mothers from traditional patriarchal families, as well as those who have chosen not to work for a period of time. Depending on local circumstances, a child care initiative could provide an invaluable practical resource for the community, as well as being a part of the Church's mission. But to do this demands a considerable time commitment and financial investment, and needs careful planning, which is why the parent and toddler group is a more realistic option for most congregations.

Many churches have had such groups for a long time, though some seem to restrict them only to 'mothers and toddlers'. Better to have one for both fathers and mothers, otherwise the Church can find itself reinforcing the impression that neither parenting nor church is for men. The fact that so many fathers attend parent and toddler groups today is something to be welcomed. It is good news for mothers, who in this generation are able to share the parenting role instead of it being their sole responsibility. And it is good news for the children, who are being given a role model for parenting that will prepare them well for being parents themselves.

So far, so good. But as we all know it is one thing to have a parent and toddler group meeting on church premises – quite another thing for it to function as an integrated part of the Church's ministry. Sometimes there are good reasons why this never happens: the Church does not really want it as part of its ministry. It can be hard to make space for babies in church. They are messy, smelly, and noisy. This explains why some churches accommodate them in the least attractive parts of their building, maybe surrounded by ancient posters of Jesus sitting with children who look quite different from themselves. One toddler we knew screamed every time he was taken to the Church creche. His parents eventually discovered that he was terrified of the premises, and to be left there was, for him, the equivalent of being abandoned on the ramparts of Count Dracula's castle. It is nothing new for small children to be problematic to the religious establishment: Jesus was born in a stable. But they are more important than that to God. And in any case, they rarely make more mess than adults: they just make a different kind of mess.

There are plenty of good resources with ideas on how to run a successful parent and toddler group from the church. But how can such a group be a genuine part of the church's mission? Most important of all, the organization and structure should always be based on a genuine partnership between those people who are part of the group. Successful and spiritually worthwhile groups are not run *by* churches *for* parents, but *in* churches *by* parents. There is a difference, and it relates to ownership and accountability. Church people like to control things, especially events attended by unchurched people. When Christians take all the responsibility, other people never feel they belong. And when people do not belong, they have no commitment. A parent and toddler group should be one of the easiest things to facilitate, but difficulties can arise in the minds of some Christians when others who seem to be non-Christian are given power to make decisions. This is an unproductive approach, for several reasons.

First, in terms of the Church's mission, it is a fact that successful evangelization most often happens through partnership and not through confrontation.[3] Secondly, a young parent with no connection with church other than a parent and toddler group is bound to have a better idea of what will suit the group than an older church member who is well-meaning (and can still play a useful part), but out of touch. And thirdly, any group in the Church ought constantly to be modelling open sharing relationships. If we cannot work together showing unconditional acceptance of other people, regardless of who they are, then our relationships will not be helpful for inspiring their own family life. Showing unconditional acceptance is not the same as doing things for people: it is about helping everyone to find their full God-given human potential. A major problem in many church groups is that there is always the ulterior motive of trying to get people to 'come to church', instead of being interested in them for who they are.

To show this level of concern, some basic information about people is obviously necessary: names, birthdays, addresses and so on. But gathering such information needs sensitivity. In one parent and toddler group we know, people did not want to divulge their addresses. Experience had predisposed them to see the Church on the side of the Establishment, and they needed to be convinced that the information obtained would not go straight to social work agencies. For them, there seemed a good chance that the Church's parent and toddler group was some sort of undercover operation to pry into their lives. It took time to break through this understandable prejudice – helped by an older granny, who knew all this information anyway because she lived in the same streets as the parents, and who was able to take the initiative in a low-key way because she was trusted and known.

Expressions of faith can play a significant part in parent and toddler groups, but this also needs sensitivity. Creative play and storytelling are likely to be more useful than singing Christian choruses. The changing seasons offer particular opportunities for celebration, and the possibility of short 'services' (though slimmed-down versions of traditional services are almost never appropriate in such a setting). In the course of our research for this book, we were startled to discover that very few clergy ever visit parent and toddler groups meeting in their churches – and that unchurched parents in these groups find that just as strange as we do.

Some of us have become so defensive about our faith that we seem almost embarrassed to mention it to anyone else at all. But when unchurched people are in a church building, they expect to encounter something to do with religion, and are surprised when they don't. That doesn't mean ministers should take things over in a pompous and paternalistic way, but conversations over coffee and Duplo can be a far more useful way of forging relationships than preaching sermons from pulpits six feet above contradiction. Small talk is no problem: most parents love to talk about their offspring. You don't need to go to every meeting of the group, or for the whole time. But a casual visit, speaking to everyone – not just church members – and taking the initiative to introduce yourself rather than waiting for formal announcements, can be a significant pastoral opportunity. If you have never tried this before, then prepare to be amazed at the number of requests for prayer you are likely to receive – and be ready to meet them!

Special Events

Not every church has the resources to run regular groups. But a seasonal event might still be possible – for instance, a storytelling or mime/movement/music group for toddlers during advent. City centre churches or those located in and around shopping malls might easily find that parents are desperate for a break from shopping, and the combination of a coffee bar with activities for the toddlers may be just what they are looking for. One church we know runs a year-round town centre shoppers' creche, and is not only providing a valuable service (for which parents pay), but also extending its own networks into many parts of the community.

As the statutory provision of pre-school facilities improves all the time, so the opportunities for churches will change. But one thing that is likely to increase in popularity is a story-telling session. Children love stories, and all over the world today there is a great rediscovery of the value of story-telling, not least because we are realizing how much we have lost in the West, by comparison with those communities which have preserved their oral traditions. Parents also love stories, and as children move just beyond the toddler stage a natural extension could be into book-borrowing facilities. Some churches have their own, others work in partnership with local libraries or schools. As governments provide ever fewer educational resources, there will be increasing demand for community groups to provide such learning experiences. Parents, of course, make good storytellers, and encouraging them in this can also enhance their experiences as parents, because all young children love to have a story read to them, and the physical closeness as a child sits on a parent's knee can play a key role in the development of a good self-image.[4]

In their book *Megatrends 2000*, John Naisbitt and Patricia Aburdene identify the growing popularity of the creative and expressive arts as one of the key features of life at the end of this century and the beginning of the next, accompanied by a decrease in the number of people actively involved in playing sports.[5] Sport is still popular, of course, and may well be a point at which churches can have useful contact with older children. But evidence of this change is already visible, and many more youngsters now want to paint, model, act and dance. The openings here are growing very fast – and, given the kind of premises that most churches have, it ought not to be too difficult for churches to help service this need.

Care after School

As children grow, so their needs change. At a time when most parents are still at work after school has ended for the day, the provision of after-school groups is a new opportunity for voluntary organizations to support family life. The image of the latchkey kid is a familiar one, and though it can be good for older children to have some home responsibilities after school, being alone can also provide the opportunity for all kinds of negative social experimentation. In any case, in Britain a child cannot legally stay at home unattended under the age of sixteen, though that is rarely enforced unless there are other circumstances that draw a child to the attention of the authorities.

The provision of appropriate after-school care is an area where churches can make a real contribution to family life. Nor need it necessarily be a drain on church finances, as many parents would be prepared to fund this kind of service. What are the advantages of such a group? Beyond the obvious one of keeping children out of mischief and danger, it can also provide useful outlets for the talents of older people, many of whom would welcome contact with youngsters once their own families are grown up or moved away. Just being available after school to sit down and hear a small child reading could make a big difference to a child who is a slow learner, or whose parents are too tired or too late when they get home from work. Nurturing families is not only about the needs of homes with children!

An after-school group needs a clearly defined aim, and for many children the provision of a space to do school homework can make a big difference to their future prospects. We have already discussed the difficulties faced by children who live in cramped homes, and who do not reach their full potential for that reason. With the rapid extension of networked computer facilities, children with no access to the Internet might be the next ones to find themselves disadvantaged, and the provision of that kind of resource could be a helpful support for them, while the constraints of the group could turn their attention away from those less desirable options which they might otherwise access. Other forms of structured learning activities, as well as the opportunity to make (and eat) snacks and teas, can help develop other skills in social interaction which often feature in school less prominently than they should.

One group of this kind operates in a very run-down and deprived area, and kids go in after school not only to do homework, but also to learn basic domestic skills. Part of their time is spent cooking an evening meal, and then when their parents come to collect them after work (mostly single mothers in this case), parents and children eat their meal together in the Church, before going off home for the evening. That is a really valuable contribution to family stability, providing very specific practical support in the form of food and skills training, all of which helps parents and children feel worth-while and valued — while just sitting at a table together creates a space for conversation that otherwise might not exist in many of their homes. In addition, all this is identifying the church as a good place to be, and thereby making a contribution to the Church's ongoing missionary task in that community.

There can be financial aid available from public service agencies for churches which can work in partnership on such schemes. Obviously, any involvement will require some commitment from a church, but it is easy to start in a small way. The scheme just described was the brainchild of only one person (a woman in her fifties), who saw a need and got it off the ground by investing her own time, and some of her own money, into it. As in all other aspects of our work with children, the child's safety must be a key concern, not just from accidents (the premises need to be safe and secure) but also from adults who might misuse their position of trust. All workers need to be thoroughly vetted and clearly under-stand the boundaries of appropriate physical contact with children, and everything that happens must be in the open and above sus-picion. But these qualifications apply to any work with children, including traditional Sunday Schools.

Parenting Groups

It is easy to think of support as something to be given in times of crisis. But when things go wrong, it is usually too late for that, and the most we can hope for then is to help minimize the damage. Far better to recognize that parents need support all the time. No matter how much experience parents might have, they are travelling a new road all the time. No two children are the same, not even in the same family, and with each one there are new lessons to be learned. At such times, it is of enormous value to be part of a group, in which parents can learn from other parents as they share their stories of life in the family. The more diverse the experiences in the group, the greater the learning is likely to be.

One particularly useful group with which we have been involved takes place once a month on Friday evenings. Several church parents were feeling the strain of family life, and what seemed to them to be conflicts between what happened in their homes and what they imagined a 'Christian family' should be like. For some, this was a pressing question because their spouses were not Christians, and this seemed to be an additional factor that could lead to tension within the home. There were also one or two single parents, together with some who were in second or subsequent marriages and who had parental responsibilities for children living in different homes. In a word, just about everybody was approaching the matter with a huge burden of guilt. This is not the ideal basis on which to establish any sort of group, but is almost inevitable in any group related to the family, because to a greater or lesser extent most parents seem to be more aware of their failures than their successes.

Some church leaders thought they knew exactly what was required, and generously offered to buy an extensive set of videos and study books produced by a Christian organization specializing in family matters. This had no appeal for us. Parenting is not like plumbing or accountancy. It is not solely a set of techniques that can be learned, but depends on a particular human identity. After delicate negotiations with church leaders we succeeded in declining their offer, and invited people to come along to the group just to meet others with the same questions as themselves, to socialize and to talk. Some in the Church thought this was a very weak agenda, but it appealed to those with the questions, and at the first meeting just under twenty people turned up. With the obvious exception of the single parents, every person came with a partner, including those whose spouses did not attend church. We also had one single (unmarried) person, who was a full-time youth and community worker, but who joined the group as an ordinary member, not in any official capacity. It was a very informal event. We started with some drinks and nibbles, and then explained what we were trying to do, and how we wanted the group to set its own agenda. But first it was important for us to share our own story of family and home. Church leaders are not good at exposing their own weaknesses, but people will never be open with us if we are not prepared to be honest with them. We just described our own family, and spoke candidly about our strengths and weaknesses as we saw them. We described the things that had not worked, as well as those that had. We also spoke about our faith, and how, when our second child died unexpectedly and suddenly, the Church and our Christian friends had been totally unable to support us. Of how we were angry and impatient with God – and of how even now, some years later, we are still puzzled and frustrated by the experience.

After that, we went round the group and each person said as much or as little as they wished. One of the things that happened has already been mentioned in chapter 2. But one feature struck us right away: the men in particular were obviously saying things that their wives had never heard them say previously! In an odd sort of way, some men seem unable to speak honestly on a one-to-one basis with their partners, but are quite happy to discuss fairly intimate details in front of a group, even one which includes their spouse!

In no time at all the group had identified an extensive agenda of shared concerns. As they were listed, it was obvious that we had been wiser than we knew in declining to use a pre-packaged programme that offered all the 'right' answers – because none of these people were asking the 'right' questions. Some matters required the insight of experts – and for those, we invited knowledgeable people to come and meet with us (but only with the agreement of the whole group as to who should be invited). At other times, we enlisted the help of older people whose children had grown up, and learned from their experience. But mostly we tackled things by sharing our own respective experiences.

What do people get out of groups like this? First of all, a chance to escape from the home and immediate demands of children. It's surprising how many parents literally never get the chance to go anywhere together. The cost of going out can be one reason; lack of reliable babysitting can be another. Parenting groups are not costly (though don't fall into the trap of providing everything for people: that only devalues them); and church should be a good place to recruit babysitters. The chance to make new friends is more significant in the lives of parents than we sometimes appreciate.

Encouragement is another important benefit: as people hear about the struggles of others, they discover that they are not alone, and it is not true that they are the worst parents in the whole world. There is the further discovery that we all have something to share. Whatever our experience, it is likely to be valuable to someone else. Some Christians can be surprised to discover that non-Christians make very good parents, and they might actually learn from them. And non-Christians can be encouraged in their search for meaning by the realization that church people have just as many struggles with families (and faith) as they have. Women who have taken time out of work for a few years to raise children are often afflicted by the 'I'm only a housewife' syndrome, and the discovery that they have something to contribute to enrich the lives of others can give a tremendous boost to their self-confidence. Mutual sharing helps us all to see we are worth something, and just to be a parent is a role of great value.

Parenting groups are also the place where people might start to come to with their own childhood. Group leaders need to be ready for this to happen, as it can often take a distressing, even violent form. As adults talk about their children, they see their own childhood experiences in a new light, maybe understanding for the first time the reasons for lost opportunities and broken relationships. When this happens, listening (as opposed to speaking) becomes even more important than normal.

This is also a point at which faith can begin to be relevant. Knowing how to include a faith dimension can be a problem for some church groups. The American psychologist Abraham Maslow once observed that 'If the only tool you have is a hammer, then you tend to see every problem as a nail'. This is supremely true of meetings in churches, where there can often be no concept of how to run anything unless it begins with a hymn and a prayer, and probably a Bible reading. If you want to kill a parenting group stone dead, then that is the way to do it. On the other hand, we are strongly of the view that faith should play a part. The precise form this takes will depend on local culture, and the personal disposition of group members and leaders. Things like parachute games or dance can be a great way to cement relationships. In our context, we would have no hesitation in using circle dances and traditional Scottish dances as part of such an evening. Different things will apply in different places, and it would be wrong for us to be prescriptive. But dance in particular has enormous potential not only for fun, but also for personal healing, in such groups. On more than one occasion, and in different countries, when we have used circle dancing focused on some kind of reflective theme people who have been the victims of sexual abuse or violence have found it addressing their personal needs in ways that other kinds of therapy seem to bypass.[6]

Thinking of fun, we have often used mask-making in groups like this – dividing into pairs and making a plaster mask on one another's faces, then talking about the experience afterwards. This is another enormously valuable tool for coming to terms with our own identity, and the way we relate to others. Some people describe the experience as like being born, others talk of being released, cleansed, or totally transformed. One woman became enraged by it, only to come back a day later and begin to address unfinished business relating to the death of her father. But we cannot emphasize too strongly the necessity for group leaders who plan to experiment with techniques as powerful as dance or mask-making to work through the possible consequences for themselves and others in advance of using them with a group.[7] Anyone wanting to explore them further would be better to enrol in a training workshop than to try them out just on the basis of having read what we have written here.

Though we would be unlikely to introduce formal prayer into a parenting group, there is great value in giving space for people to be prayed with. Surprisingly, you might easily find that unchurched people are more receptive to this than those who are regular attenders! If a group includes non-Christians, then don't try and convert them, but equally don't be embarrassed to offer to pray with them when they face particular challenges (though always ask first: never pray uninvited).

Parenting groups can also play an important part in the Church's mission. A friend of ours began a group with eight couples, with the idea that after some time they in turn would network with other couples and be available to run groups themselves. These groups had a snowball effect and proved so popular they found themselves invited by the local school board to run them in the school as well as the church.

Some churches run groups for parents who are divorced, and working through how to be a good parent when children live with former spouses. Others have groups for those struggling with the demands of being an acceptable parent in a blended family, or for single parents, victims of abuse, or families in conflict with the law. Variations on the theme are endless. Sometimes it makes good sense for a group to comprise people from all these different parenting situations, but quite often – either through prejudice or because of the need for specialist help or just because of sheer numbers – separate provision makes more sense.

Incidentally, to do any in-depth work a group needs at least three people, and probably not more than eight to ten. In a church with several groups, it is always a good thing for them to meet together at least now and again. The advantage of meeting people who have the same problem or situation is that you can empathize very readily with one another. Just knowing that other people have the same difficulties can be sufficient help, while hearing how someone else has handled them can also be a great encouragement. The disadvantage is that a group of people who are all the same can become claustrophobic. The crucial point to remember is the need to be flexible. Groups should be in a continual state of change anyway, because hopefully the needs and concerns of the people in them will change. If they don't, then the group isn't serving a purpose! And eventually, all groups come to an end.

In any group situation, it is important for group facilitators to remember that they are just that: they are not counsellors. They need to be open and sensitive to other people, and know where to find specialist help for particular individuals as and when that may be needed. Training for group facilitators is obviously important, and can be done very effectively not by hand-picking people who seem to be natural leaders, but by offering it to everyone. A course in reflective listening can be particularly useful, and the skills picked up during such training might actually be the very thing many people are lacking in terms of their own family relationships. The more people who have these skills, the more effective the group will be anyway. Training of this sort could profitably be done ecumenically – indeed much of this kind of support work could also be done very effectively in that context.

Groups can start in a small way. Many emerge out of counselling situations, as clergy and others become aware of different people with similar needs, and put them in touch with each other. Some groups may well not want to broadcast their existence, and sensitivity to this is important.

Some Christians seem to imagine that just being a Christian empowers people to handle every conceivable eventuality in life. But parenting skills need to be learned. Few of us are well equipped, and we generally pass on the sort of parenting we have received. Most people want to be good parents. No-one plans to make mistakes. But stresses along the way often mean that is what happens. It can be difficult to change, even if we want to. Unfortunately, some mistakes are not easily put right, and children can be left with severe personality disorders. Parenting groups will not prevent all the mistakes, but they will enable people to change some things, and above all they create a safe space for parents to admit they need help – and to find it. That is probably the single most valuable contribution that any church can make to family support.

Personal Growth and Faith Development

If childhood shapes adult people, then parents need to learn about child development and understand the role they will play in their child's life. For most, this learning will also be part of their own self-discovery, because personal faith development is a lifelong process for us all.[8] Certainly, understanding our first child's spiritual growth led us into a much fuller recognition of what it means to have faith, and to be nurtured within the Christian community. In his ground-breaking book *Will Our Children Have Faith?* Christian educator John H. Westerhoff III used the illustration of a tree to describe how a child's faith develops. A tree grows by adding rings — yet is still a real tree no matter how few rings it has — and a child's faith is just the same. Moreover, just as a tree takes its character from the parent tree, so children learn faith from their parents. A child's first learning experiences about anything are not cognitive or intellectual, but related to senses such as touch, taste, and smell. Faith, he argued, is the same: children learn what God is like by getting to know their parents. For a small child, what the parent is will determine what God is. There is no space here to elaborate on this understanding of how faith develops, except to say that in practical terms it places a great value on the relationships that develop between parent and child. Particularly in the evangelical tradition, some parents expend inordinate amounts of energy in the effort to 'convert' their children, whom they perceive as little pagans, when it would be of more long-term benefit if they were to concentrate on being good parents.[9]

For parents who have divorced, this is a hard challenge, especially for divorced fathers who are usually the ones who end up living separately from their children. With the best will in the world, it is not easy for fathers in that situation to keep up with their children and to continue being good fathers. Western society has simply not thought through this issue.[10] While court judgments restricting access by fathers to their children are often made for good reasons, especially when violence and abuse have been involved, to imagine that adequate fathering can take place in just a few hours at weekends flies in the face of all the facts. Many noncustodial parents just give up on it, and no more than about one in six of fathers who are entitled to regular access actually take up the option. Even those who do all too easily become a figure who spends money on their children, indiscriminately giving them treats that can make it even more difficult for the mother, who is responsible for all the hard work of day-to-day parenting. Working out how to help absent parents to be real parents, who offer constant advice and discipline, is not going to be easy. Some churches have begun to explore this area, through providing a safe neutral territory on which fathers can meet their children. Particularly in cases where abuse has been an issue, there may be a legal requirement for supervised access. That is a good start, but this can be progressed further by the development of fatherhood groups, at which fathers and their children meet with facilitators and do things as varied as sports or trips to the cinema or country. Doing things in a group is itself a good experience in learning relational skills, and in the USA (where only 51% of children now live with both their biological parents) this kind of group activity has been shown to make a significant contribution to other social problems afflicting the lives of single parents, such as unemployment, alcoholism and drug addiction.[11]

There is a similar need for safe places in which families that have suffered abuse can begin to learn to be together again. Public agencies have limited resources for such provision, but a warm, comfortable space where families can sit and play, as well as cook a meal together, can make a major contribution to family healing. Sitting and talking at such a time can be very difficult: doing things together can start the process of a return to normal relationships. This is something that would need to be done in collaboration with statutory social work agencies, but they are generally very welcoming to approaches from churches along these lines.

Many parents are concerned about how to protect their children from sexual abuse. Several organizations offer useful material in this area, though without doubt the most outstanding are the courses developed through the innovative work of the Rev. Marie M. Fortune at the Center for the Prevention of Sexual and Domestic Violence in Seattle. Her course for nine to twelve year olds, packaged and intended to be used in the same way as traditional Sunday School or Vacation Bible School materials, is one that could be offered with great advantage.[12] There is an opportunity here for churches with vision and imagination to provide a resource that would receive strong support from many other non-church organizations, and which could provide yet another point of bridgebuilding into the wider community.

Problems over drug abuse and experimentation should also

feature on the Church's agenda, because part of our responsibility to children is to ensure that – without causing them undue fear – they are well-informed and know how to handle the kind of difficult situations which some will meet even in primary school. Partnerships with schools could easily be the way to work in this area: many schools just have insufficient resources to handle all the problems, while many teachers themselves have no idea what to say. The local situation will determine the way forward, but Christians certainly have a contribution to make. Here, as everywhere else in ministering to families, prevention is better than cure. In most pastoral situations, churches tend to be reactive, waiting for a crisis to occur and then trying to pick up the pieces. We are often quite good at doing this, but to be of maximum usefulness both to our own members and to the wider community (of which Christians are also a part), we will need to give much higher priority to taking initiatives that will sustain and support family life at the point before real problems arise.

8

FROM TEENAGE TO THIRD AGE

Teenagers

Children do not stay the same for long. As sure as day follows night, they are changing all the time. But some changes are more significant than others, and the transition from childhood to teenage can be one of the most traumatic. Though the foundation of mature adulthood will have been laid long before a child hits the magic age of thirteen, it is during the teenage years that decisions about all kinds of significant issues begin to be made. Young people at this stage of life can be hard to understand, and it is frequently a time of great turmoil – for themselves as individuals, as well as in relation to their parents and the wider family circle. On the one hand, teenagers want to look as though they have it all together, yet on the other they are uncertain of themselves and need support. They want to be financially independent, and yet are generally unable to provide for themselves, either because they want to have the opportunity of further education, or because they are unable to get it and find themselves unemployed. They want to forge adult relationships, yet find it hard to handle the emotional tensions that they can create.

All adults have been teenagers, and yet this is the one age group that parents typically feel least able to relate to. We have been parents of a teenager since 1982, and it will be 2002 before our youngest child leaves the teenage years. During that period, we have reflected many times on what teenagers need from their parents. A lot of things have changed, including the nature of teenage itself. One thing is constant: the difficulties some families encounter at this time are often not with the teenagers, but with the parents. Life in the family always requires that we be open about our own attitudes, and honest about our weaknesses as well as grateful for our strengths. When our children are younger and more dependent, it is relatively easy to control things in such a way that we are rarely personally challenged. But the teenage years bring us face-to-face with ourselves in a way that can provide parents with exciting opportunities for personal growth – as well as the possibility of total family disintegration.

Parenting Teenagers

No one can talk about teenagers without mentioning music. Different generations have always had a love-hate relationship with one another's music. But it is not just about musical preferences. Have you noticed how teenagers can seem to have no interest in talking with their parents, and when asked a question they will simply grunt or give a dismissive reply – and continue listening to music. Music is a language, and at a time in life when it is hard to articulate your own thoughts, listening to music can be an important way of working things through. We have all had the experience of hearing someone else say something, and realize that their words reflected our own feelings, but we would never have been able to say it like that. By taking time to listen to their music, parents can learn a lot of things that teenagers would like to say to them. It is important not to dismiss something just because you can't understand it. Far better to begin to listen and to dialogue.

The problem for parents is that even the rules of dialogue are changing all the time. The actual way that today's teenagers communicate and process information is quite different from what it was only one generation ago. Our own children cover a wide range of ages, and the oldest was already a teenager when our youngest was born. To a significant extent, the world in which our older son grew up was not so very different from how it had been in our own teenage years. In terms of communication, books were still a major learning tool, talking with someone else generally occupied a person's whole attention, and the modern electronics industry was in its infancy. Today all that has changed. Our youngest child can do homework, listen to music, play with a computer game, eat a meal, watch the TV, and carry on a conversation – all at the same time. It can be disconcerting for older people to realize that doing this makes no difference to her level of achievement. The actual ways in which teenagers communicate are changing, and parents need to appreciate this, and be a part of the new style. Instead of insisting, for example, that everything else be abandoned to hold a conversation, we need to allow our teenagers to do more than one thing at once, and to be aware that they are likely to be much better at doing it than we are. Trying to make them as we once were will be a recipe for unnecessary confrontation, and can provoke crisis, not avert it.

Another thing parents need to remember is that our children learn their behaviour from us. The older they get, the more like us they become, and the more adult they seem then the more threatening it can be to have your own behavioural patterns reflected in someone else. Some parents dislike their teenagers because they dislike themselves. If during their children's formative years, parents have established a pattern of physical or verbal abuse as the way to make things happen in the home, then they can be sure their teenagers will imitate them with a vengeance – and it will not be a pleasurable experience to be on the receiving end. On the other hand, a family where open and loving communication networks have been in place from the start – particularly in relation to parents being prepared to listen to children as well as speak to them – will invariably reap the benefits when teenage comes.

Adults regularly find themselves parents of teenagers at a time when their own lives are under pressure for other reasons, and this can also affect the way they relate to their own children. Obviously, the age of teenagers' parents depends on their age when their children were born, and that is going to be different for each child in a family. But it is generally the case that parents of teenagers are in mid-life, and this can be a challenging time anyway. Mid-life crisis may be difficult to describe in any hard-and-fast way, as different people evolve different ways of handling their own ageing. But at some time between the ages of about forty and fifty-five, our perceptions of life do tend to change, and some people have a real struggle to cope. By this time, adults often feel they have achieved whatever significant things they are going to do in life. If they have missed that important promotion at work, then they are probably never going to get it. If they passed by the opportunity to move to a different town or country, it will not come their way again. If they never got around to conceiving that other child they had vaguely dreamed about having, then they have lost the chance. In addition, some experience a general lack of vitality, and a greater awareness of their own mortality. Some problem areas can be physiological, and largely beyond the control of both teenagers and their parents. If you combine the emotional turmoil of an adolescent with the mood swings of a menopausal mother and of a mid-life father, then by any definition you have an explosive mixture. In all these things, the diminishing possibilities for parents can provide a stark contrast with the increasing potential of their own teenagers. Teenagers, with the whole of life before them, can remind us of who we once were – and the lost opportunities that we may still hanker for. At such a time, the natural instinct can be to preserve the status quo in as many areas of life as possible. This no doubt explains why in church life it is usually the middle-aged (men in particular) who are afraid of change, and not the elderly. But in the family, at the very time that parents can themselves be struggling with rapid change, their teenage offspring are also changing very fast.

Adults handle mid-life in many different ways, no doubt related to their own temperament and previous experience. But for those who are insecure at this time, the maturing of their children can be exceedingly threatening to their own personal sense of identity and self-worth. The natural instinct might be to try to control and restrict our offspring in an authoritarian way – in effect, to try to keep things the same by preventing them from growing up. That is never a good idea at any stage, but whereas parents with a patriarchal attitude can at least make it look as if it works in early childhood,

having a domineering parent as a teenager can lead to a total breakdown in family relationships. A breakdown at this stage frequently
lasts well into adult life, and it can take many years to repair the
damage.

Just to add to the problems of parents, some will find themselves
forced to care for their ageing parents at exactly the same time as
they are trying to handle their own children's teenage years. This can
also coincide with financial pressures, which may seem to be exacerbated by the fact that teenagers (inevitably) cost more to clothe and
feed than smaller children, not to mention the incessant pressure to
be always buying the latest trendy gear.

Some parents will handle all this better than others. Those who
are prepared to work through these and similar issues will almost
always find themselves emerging as better people, for their own
partners as well as for their children – while those who refuse to
come to grips with their own personal baggage at this time are likely
to find a progressive deterioration in all aspects of relationships in
the home. Increasing numbers of marriages break up when parents
are struggling with teenage offspring. But even the most open families can use all the support they can get at this time. The whole
ethos of church life can make a major contribution, and in chapter 6
we have already noted the damage that can be caused by an
unhealthy emphasis on sin and guilt in the worship and preaching of
the church. Churches which have support groups in place will
already have a major asset to help parents handle the teenage years.
As well as enabling parents who may be struggling with mid-life to
share something of their accumulated wisdom with younger parents
(something that will enhance their self-image anyway), many of the
younger parents in such a group will not be far away from their own
teenage years, and will be able to reflect on how they managed to
cope, and what things made a difference.

Teenagers and Church

Teenagers also need support. In particular, they need to be accepted
in the Church and to be taken seriously by other adults. If teenagers

do not feel they belong, then they are unlikely to develop any lasting and worthwhile relationships with the Church. In this respect, they are fundamentally no different from any other age group, except that in adolescence the need to belong and be accepted and affirmed in one's new, emerging adult personality is much stronger than it is at almost any other time of life. One of the great tragedies of most Western churches is the way children who have been nurtured within Christian families tend to fall away from faith during early teenage. The reasons for this are complex, but there is no question that if teenagers do not feel they belong, then they will not stay. Why should they? Kim Philby was one of the most damaging double agents in the British intelligence service during the twentieth century. Years after selling his country's secrets, and defecting to live in the old Soviet Union, he was asked why he had done it. His answer was simple, yet revealing: 'I never really felt I belonged in England'. The sense of belonging and being accepted and valued is absolutely central to the development of teenagers into mature adults. It is also the most relevant factor in attracting teenagers to the Church, and keeping them there. In terms of the church's mission, the numerical decline of Christianity in the West could be reversed overnight if the churches could only keep those children who grow up within church families. They leave because all too often the Church places all the emphasis on believing the right things, and little or no emphasis on the importance of community. But belonging will always precede believing, and experiencing acceptance comes well before any theological or doctrinal reflection.

This sense of belonging can be engendered in many different ways, some of them obvious. For example, if teenagers never hear people like them referred to in the prayers in church services, they can be forgiven for supposing they do not belong. Yet they are mentioned only infrequently. If people of their own age never take part in the service, then it should not surprise us if they fail to attend. On the other hand, when they are recognized and their skills are used, they will be there. Teenagers can do many things very effectively. Some things they may do better than adults, such as operating the PA system or providing the regular musical accompaniment. They can also have a relevant input into the leadership structures of the church. It can be depressing to hear of church committees searching for young people to join them, and defining 'young' as people in their late twenties or thirties. Of course, young people are not necessarily going to be available to attend meetings at the times that suit older people – and they will certainly be unlikely to make church committees a major priority at this stage in their life. But churches that do not share decision-making and responsibility with young people need not be surprised if they lose them. Teenagers will be in church when they know they are needed. Churches which have taken seriously what was said in a previous chapter about the creation of family-friendly churches will have fewer problems in this regard.

What church can provide most of all is the support of a group. Parents are not the only ones who can be helped by being part of a support group. If anything, the company of peers is even more important for teenagers than it is for their parents. But teenage is not just one single state of being. In time, the teenage years are relatively short, and only last from thirteen to nineteen. But they span a colossal range of human development, both physical and personal. Most sixteen year olds feel they have little in common with fourteen year olds, while someone of nineteen is entirely different from a thirteen year old. Teenagers between twelve and fourteen or fifteen need to have the opportunity to be with others of the same age, but not be pressured by older teenagers. A group of fifteen to seventeen or twenty year olds will have a different agenda, and young people of that age also need the space to explore questions relevant to them without being held back by younger teens. To accommodate this, the most effective youth groups will be changing all the time, as different ages and stages predominate in the life of a particular congregation. But there are some general considerations that apply at all stages of teenage.

As with any other kind of support group, the choice of leaders for a youth group is crucial. It is always important to have more than one leader, including both women and men. Churches sometimes choose youth leaders because they are interested in music, but people skills are much more important. The way leaders relate to each other will provide an important role model for teenagers, and in some circumstances one or two young married couples can be ideal. Some of the very best youth groups we know are run by people like this. On the other hand, so are some of the worst. Churches can impose unfair responsibilities on couples who are themselves at a formative stage in their own relationships, and that is counterproductive both for the group and the couple. In addition, many of the people who fall into this category are pursuing demanding careers, and need to maximize their own opportunities for rest and relaxation. Couples without children also have the freedom to make spontaneous decisions about how they will spend their leisure, and doing so does not always work to the advantage of teenagers with whom they may be involved. When a youth group is focused around the leaders' own lifestyles, then teenagers (who of course can be notoriously fickle themselves) will feel let down. In such demanding work, flexibility needs to be combined with a serious level of commitment. It is a costly and time-consuming business to be available to teenagers, and those who take on such work need to be prepared for that. In the end, commitment is far more important than age. Some of the best youth groups are run by people well past mid-life, though if older people get involved it is important that they be themselves, and do not try to use a youth group as a way of hanging onto the last vestiges of their own youth. There is nothing worse than a group for teenagers run by trendy fifty–year–olds who are obviously well past their sell-by date. Incidentally, always remember that young people can minister to young people. A church in Seattle has a regular programme to pair up teenagers with someone else who is only one or (at most) two years older than themselves. They befriend one another, go places together, learn new skills together – and encourage each other in faith and growing up, as they share what they are learning.

In terms of programme, a major mistake is to run a youth group as if it was an extension of formal education. The eminent German theologian Emil Brunner once commented that 'The Church lost its way when it substituted the model of the classroom for the model of community' – a theme which we have emphasized repeatedly throughout this book. All young people are good at something, and the recognition of their skills helps them to feel valued. Many of them could be used in the context of the wider church community, and any activity which involves working alongside other people will always make a significant contribution to the personal development of teenagers (and others who get involved). In the ideal scenario, the Church should provide two different kinds of activity for each of the adolescent age bands we have identified: a group for fun and friendship, and another for learning and discipleship.

Still, school does occupy a large chunk of a young teenager's life, and this can easily develop into a friction point between church and home. Responsible parents will not appreciate it when the Church always holds youth events late on Sunday evenings, thereby making it more difficult for teenagers to get up in good time for school the next day. With an imaginative approach, the integration of school work with recreation can provide useful opportunities for the Church to support teenagers. Many Australian churches run special swot camps for their young people, in the school holiday immediately preceding the main annual examinations. The kids take their work to camp, and have organized times to do exam preparation, backed up with skilled assistance from Christians with specialist knowledge of particular subjects. Having a structure helps them get more work done than if they were at home by themselves (and overcomes the loneliness of study), while it also provides space for play and relaxation as well as faith building. The kids like it, their parents are willing to pay for it, and older generations of church members find a useful outlet for their talents. In the process, teenagers are exploring at first hand a collaborative model of working that can only be enormously beneficial to them. The residential model may not work everywhere, but the needs of teenagers for space to do their school homework is just as pressing as the needs of younger children. Some of the ideas we mentioned in the last chapter could easily be adapted to suit this older age group.'

Teenagers and Sex

Music, communication, and education fade into insignificance for many teenagers when compared with their discovery of the opposite sex. Teenagers today have more freedom to explore this openly than was once the case, and the predominance of mixed-sex schools has helped to explode many fantasies, as well as to present new temptations. Teenagers are constantly adjusting to their own physical maturity, but that does not stop many young people being sexually active while still at school. Indeed, in the absence of any appropriate guidance from most churches and many homes, sexual experimentation becomes an important way of coming to terms with the physical changes which are taking place. Despite the resources poured into sex education by school authorities, young people still frequently take their information and values from their peers, whose ideas and experiences might in turn have been taken from anywhere.

The Church has always had a problem with sex.[2] It is a deep-rooted problem, because its origins are in a general unease with the body as a whole. It was the Gnostics in the second century who first argued that the only thing that really matters is a person's spiritual spark, and though they were heretics many otherwise orthodox Christians have agreed with them. If the body is irrelevant to Christian faith and spirituality, you do one of two things with it: either you starve it, by living a very ascetic lifestyle, or you indulge it on the pretext that if it is of no importance, then how it is used makes no difference anyway. Both attitudes can be found in the modern church, and neither is particularly helpful. The trouble is that the Church adopts a very narrow attitude to sex, and typically invests much more energy in condemning what is regarded as illicit sex than in promoting a healthy approach to sexuality. Since sex is an inescapable fact of life, in the absence of positive role models or discussion about it teenagers will tend to do it without any reference to wider Christian values, not because they don't care but because they have no access to what these Christian values might be anyway. For teenagers who discover they are homosexual, the difficulty is only magnified, and they might find no opportunities at all for self-discovery and values–formation within the Church.[3]

There are no slick answers to these questions, and many adults will prefer not to address them at all, largely because of their own hang-ups about the subject. But young people need space to explore all sorts of topics. Parents have a part to play in making space for conversation, and not hiding behind a newspaper or being continually too busy to talk. The Church also needs to create space for teenagers to explore such issues with other teenagers, and with responsible leaders who can and do model good practice in their own lives. Of course, the real heart of the matter is not sex, but relationships. Young people will forge relationships, and the choice for the faith community is how to facilitate and support them in this. Here, as in most other areas of ministering to families, the one vital ingredient will be the creation of safe spaces where they can meet with their friends without embarrassment, knowing that they will be received and welcomed with no conditions attached. And a place where they can interact with leaders who will not be easily shocked or surprised, who can support and stand alongside them, while at the same time gently pointing them to the values of the Gospel.

In the USA, some very encouraging experiments have taken place in the public education system, by including classes on parenting for teenagers. These have been so successful that eight states now make these classes a requirement for high school graduation, and others are likely to follow suit. It will be a long time before every teenager can expect to have such provision in high school, but this is an area in which the Church could easily provide a valuable resource. One of the difficulties in running a teenage group in church is finding helpful ways to address young people's questions. Many churches take a traditionalist (and easy) way out, by providing opportunities for Bible study. Examining the issues of parenting can help at different points in the teenage years. It might seem that parenthood is a long way off for a child of fourteen, but working through issues of discipline or child development can be useful for a teenager who coaches a football team, or whose younger siblings are always asking difficult questions. In addition, drawing up a family budget or watching a film on childbirth can bring an air of reality to discussions on sex, and make a significant contribution to the avoidance of the possibility of teenage pregnancies.[4]

Making Connections

The point at which teenage turns into young adulthood is somewhat indeterminate. Our own experience is less than typical as we fell in love in our late teenage years and got married to each other as soon as we were no longer teenagers. The fact that we are still married – and in love – more than a quarter of a century later only shows that relationships do not follow one universal and predictable pattern. When we chose to marry at such a young age, our decision was accompanied by all sorts of warnings about the dire consequences that were likely to follow. Though none of them subsequently admitted it, it is a fair guess that most of our relatives did not expect our relationship to last. They had good reason for such doubts, because in statistical terms young marriages have a high failure rate. We just happened to be the lucky ones.

In the West, the age at which young people choose to get married is actually increasing. The economic pressures to marry earlier are no longer relevant, while there is a wider choice of living styles available than was once the case. At one time, the only way for a young person to leave the parental home was through marriage. Nowadays it is a normal part of growing up for young people to share accommodation with others of their own age, while the greater acceptability of cohabiting means that many people live together before thinking about marriage, while some make this a lifelong arrangement.

Christians may wish to engage in all kinds of extensive theological and moral debates on such issues. But in terms of practical ministry, one of the most helpful things the Church can do for young adults who are forging what will hopefully be lifetime relationships is to make space for them to reflect on some of the challenges that are likely to occur when two people from different family backgrounds share a home and relationship together. So far, we have emphasized the value of support groups in church life, but this is one exception to that general rule. When comparing the experiences of churches that offer group activities to those thinking of marriage with those which deal with each couple separately, then the second pattern always seems to win hands down. Everyone needs some broad frame of reference within which to make relationships, but every actual relationship is individual and special, and especially at this exploratory stage can best be worked through in a less public way.

It is amazing how many churches still offer absolutely nothing by way of advice or counselling, and listening, to couples thinking of marriage. This is yet another instance where it is easy to speak in one way and act in another. Churches which claim to be concerned with the rising incidence of marriage failure, yet do nothing to help couples work through things in advance, lack credibility. Even when some kind of advice is on offer, it frequently relates only to the organizational details of a wedding, and not to the more important relational aspects of marriage. Part of the reason is that clergy often think they need to do everything. When their main concern is the actual conduct of a service it is unsurprising that this is where much of their attention is concentrated. In reality, marriage preparation is an obvious subject where the clergy are not necessarily going to be the best people, and lay people can have a lot to contribute.

Ideally, a couple contemplating marriage can be linked some months before the wedding with another person or persons who will help them work through the demands they will face in different aspects of their relationship. Married couples do not always make the best guides in this respect, as it is easy for them to tell others how it should be (based on their own experience), rather than facilitating genuine exploration. Every relationship is different, and a single person can often be a very good facilitator. Since those who are getting married are always single, arguably another single person will have more in common with them. Childless couples also potentially have much to contribute here. Not only are they likely to have more time available than a couple with young children, but because of their childlessness they will almost certainly have been forced to pay more attention to the actual working-out of their own relationship. Couples looking forward to marriage need help to recognize the personal baggage that each will bring to the relationship, and the likely consequences of that. This might include the addressing of some deep-seated hang-ups related to their past. It will normally involve some kind of personality analysis, to help them find out who they really are.

There also needs to be discussion of questions such as 'How will I react if my partner . . . ?' When couples have worked through ways of handling possible conflict situations in advance, then when conflict arises they have some common ground on which to begin resolving it. The issue of domestic violence and its consequences should also be included here. Beyond that, there are all the realities of everyday life together, as well as issues about possible parenthood, which may seem a long way off, but needs to be tackled at this stage. What sort of family would they like to be? What about finance? Who would look after any children? Would it be practical for one parent to take leave or give up work? Would they share parental leave? If both of them were to return to work, how would they want their child to be looked after? If by a third party, then who might it be? What sort of care would they be expecting or wanting, and what about parental bonding or spiritual role models? The answers given to these and other questions will vary depending on each couple's circumstances, and some of them might seem premature questions in advance of marriage. But raising them at this stage is always going to be worthwhile, as these are the issues on which relationships can founder. Talking things through sooner rather than later can help establish a pattern of communication that will be invaluable when real conflict arises (as it will). Many marriages fail not because couples are incompatible, or their problems insoluble, but because they have no idea how to talk openly with one another.

What we have said so far has assumed that marriage is between two young adults, getting married for the first time. But people marry at many other points in life, including those who marry for the first time at an older age as well as those whose previous marriages have ended through death or divorce. It is a mistake to imagine that older people have no problems to work through: they may actually have more, especially if each partner has children and they are trying to create a blended family. The questions are bound to be different, but the Church should provide the same facility for these people as we have just described for younger couples. The question of remarriage in church will provoke agitated debate in some quarters. It is a matter of regret that some denominations have made this a matter of church policy and as a result have left themselves with little or no flexibility in such affairs. But so far as pastoral support for the family is concerned, the answer is always going to be found in offering acceptance and affirmation to those wanting to make commitments to one another. The fact is that today, when cohabitation is increasingly becoming more popular, *anyone* wanting to be married is making a significant statement.

Given the radical changes that have taken place in the whole of Western culture in recent years, merely looking back to what churches did fifty years ago is an irrelevance. We are in a new situation, and we need to start from the realities of that. In a world which is increasingly lonely and hostile, there is less and less support being offered to those who want to follow Christian values. It is hypocritical to proclaim the virtues of lifelong commitments if we are unprepared to provide the infrastructure that will support people who want to make such commitments. The good intentions may not always work out, but neither will many other resolutions we make in the effort to live by the values of God's kingdom. The Gospel, however, takes account of that, and bearing the cross of failure and despair is but the prelude to celebrating the new life of resurrection. When the Church is a real community, both cross-bearing and empowerment are both equally community responsibilities.

Newly-weds need time to get to know each other. It's a time for the Church to give rather than to see them as new potential leaders. During our first two years of marriage, we were greatly blessed by belonging to a congregation where we were often invited out for Sunday lunch. It was only years later that we realized what a great help that had been. In our tight working schedule, it relieved one of the pressure points of our week, saved us some money (which was important at the time), as well as giving us a good reason to keep going to church too, while the conversation and company gave us a sense of value.

Support for couples is not something that should end with marriage. In the previous chapter, we said a good deal about support for parents – but parents also have ongoing relationships with each other, not just with their children. One of the major contributing factors to marital dysfunction is the way in which adults' lives can be consumed by their children, to the detriment of their own personal development (and ultimately, that also affects their effectiveness as parents). Relationships are tender plants, and they do not grow without being nurtured, particularly in the changing context of modern family life where parents have so many demands placed on their time and energy – demands that are only multiplied where there have been previous marriages and other sets of children to be supported. Between paid work and housework, leisure and parenting, it can be impossible to keep all the balls in the air at once. Church people, especially clergy, can have other demands imposed by the incessant round of meetings that most churches seem to believe are essential for spiritual growth. There is no doubt that, at this point, being committed to the church can seriously damage your family life. Clergy can do themselves and their churches a big favour by being open enough about their own struggles to be willing to join as members (not leaders) of such a group that is focused on relationships between couples.

A brief word about single people is in order here. We make no apology for not having said much on this theme. In a book of this size, it is impossible to cover everything, and a book on the family naturally needs to concentrate primarily on the home as a community of several people. Nevertheless, many people never marry, and all this talk of the Church needing to be family-friendly and provide support groups for parents can be alienating. The key to overcoming some of this resentment is for the Church to be a genuine community, with space for growth and friendship to continue between those who are married and those who are not. Each group brings different strengths and insights, which can enrich the whole community. Though the Bible has a lot to say about marriage, it also makes it clear that marriage is not the purpose of human life. All people are made in the image of God, and our major purpose is to reflect and serve God. That means being single is as important and significant a position as being married, and in the context of family ministries there can be a significant place for single people. In the parenting group of which we wrote in the last chapter, for example, one single man regularly attended and made contributions that often helped the parents not to take themselves too seriously, while the one person who has made the most significant contribution to our own son's spiritual development is a single person who befriended him at an early age and has had the commitment to carry that friendship through his teenage years and beyond.

Third Age

One of the inescapable facts about Western society is that the average age of our people is getting older all the time. Some consequences of this are already beginning to make themselves felt, as governments struggle to find sufficient resources to put into health care, domestic help in the home, and social services for the elderly. Benefits that a generation ago were taken for granted are now being eroded, as the working population shrinks and there is less money available to pay for things. People who are now middle-aged might well find that by the time they retire a state retirement pension is non-existent, or so seriously eroded in value that it will provide no useful level of financial security.

Older people can play an important part in family life, and historically have always done so all around the world.[5] The extended family in which several generations lived in close proximity and supported one another could be suffocating for younger people, who never had a chance to discover and develop their own identity. On the other hand, at its best it provided many of the networks of support and counselling for which people now need to consult professional agencies. Some of the problems which people now expect to sort out with the aid of professional therapists are the kind of questions that, in a previous generation, would have been addressed in an informal way through consultations with grandparents and others in the wider family circle. Many of the difficulties over child care that confront today's parents would have been handled by grandparents in the past.

Sometimes, they still are, and there is a growing trend for working parents to leave their children in the care of their own parents. This can be an ideal arrangement when it works, but it can also be a recipe for disaster, if grandparents do not share the same values and ideals as their own children. Nor should we forget that the extended family was and is often based on repressive patriarchal structures, in which violence and abuse can flourish and remain hidden.

Increased mobility in our society has created problems for older people. The majority no longer have the option to be part of an extended family network, even if they wish to be. Younger generations move away from the parental home, following education or employment, and many find themselves separated from their own children and their grandchildren by long distances. Coupled with changing patterns of work, this means that people in their fifties and sixties who still have plenty of energy and a lot to offer, can find themselves isolated and struggling to make a contribution to the next generations. People in this stage of life – what is generally called the 'third age' – will be a major resource for the Church in the next few years. Affirming them will not only bring benefits to their own home life, but can also be a major contributory factor in the development of the local congregation as a genuine community which has space for all ages. The establishment of relationships between older and younger couples can be to the advantage of both. The same reasons related to work and travel that separate grandparents from their own biologically-related grandchildren also mean that many children are separated from their own grandparents. Moreover, in families which have experienced multiple divorce and remarriage, children are struggling to know who they are and with whom they belong. In such circumstances, grandparents – whether related or surrogate – are likely to be invaluable. In an ideal world – and church – no doubt such relationships would be forged naturally. In reality, it might be necessary for churches to foster their development through some more formal means.

The skills of such people can readily be used in other ways we have already touched on, for instance in work with teenagers (particularly in the context of the swot camp). But a church with a concern for the whole family can also provide appropriate resources to meet the needs of older people more directly. It is not only families with children that can suffer from lack of space at home. Older people frequently have the same problem, which in their case can be exacerbated by loneliness. The equivalent of parent and toddler groups and parenting groups, but for older people, can be very welcome. The principles of providing physical and psychological space are the same at every age: it is never satisfactory just to sit people down and do everything for them. That way we devalue them, which is the exact opposite of what the Gospel is about. People prefer to be involved and useful, and when we facilitate that we are enhancing their quality of life as well as reflecting Gospel values. Sometimes intergenerational groups may be appropriate. Craft groups are very popular in Australian churches. Those who have particular skills share them with others, who for their part are eager to learn new things. Even quite small churches can easily have 100 people at a craft group. In one we visited, two old ladies in their nineties sat and played Scrabble, while at the other end of the age range young mothers with children made clothes, while others were caring for their children. This particular group operates on the basis of 'show what you know': patchwork, calligraphy, stencilling, woodwork, knitting, sewing, picture framing – the list is endless. It is, in effect, re-creating something like the extended family, but through voluntary association. In the process, lonely people find friendship, and relationships are established that lead to mutual encouragement for people at different stages of family life. Meanwhile, those who may be searching for the relevance of faith to it all can see acceptance and unconditional love in action, and be challenged to follow Jesus.

It is easy for Christians to regret the family dysfunction that many people are experiencing today. But our churches have rich resources which, with imagination and vision, can be used to empower and renew the family. Our buildings are part of that resource, just as a home is an important asset for a family. But people are the most valuable resource of all. The one thing we all have in common, at whatever stage of life and family experience we may find ourselves, is our humanity. In his book *Living the Faith Community*, John Westerhoff remarks that 'we commonly think of Christian life from an individualistic or, at best, an organizational perspective, but rarely from a communal perspective'.[6] In that respect, we share the weakness of our culture, where individualism and structures have taken over, and the result is a lot of lonely and battered people. It is no wonder that families are struggling to be communities, because we are presenting them with so few viable models. When the Church models new ways of living and relating to one another in an inclusive community that spans all generations and has space for all kinds of people, that may be the most valuable contribution we can make to the revitalization of the family in our generation.

9

MINISTERING TO FAMILIES IN CRISIS

Families find themselves in crisis for many different reasons. Terminal illness and death affect both parents and children; divorce can occur; children and adults may find themselves struggling with disabilities; one or more members of a family can find themselves in hospital, or involved in a serious accident. The list is endless, and to cover all such eventualities would need another book to itself. Most of the examples just mentioned are dealt with elsewhere in this series of *Handbooks of Pastoral Care*.

But there are some significant forms of family crisis that arise out of the dynamic of family life itself, as one member of a family tries to manipulate relationships in the home for their own personal advantage. Many people suffer in silence behind the closed doors of their homes, yet are unable to share their concerns with others because their experiences are too painful. Violent abuse within the family is a major problem, and every church, however small, is likely to have several people who have suffered this way or who will do so at some stage of their life. It can create real problems for the Church. Part of the problem is that church structures have insufficient open spaces within which people can easily share their experiences with other Christians. Support groups of the sort we have already described can help. But because of the general conspiracy of silence, by the time an issue relating to domestic violence and abuse surfaces in the Church, it is likely to have reached serious proportions. When that happens, it is important that church leaders know what they are going to do about it. If a person in distress comes to the Church office looking for help in a situation of abuse, that is not the time to start finding out how to handle it. There should be a set of procedures in place so that the Church can give immediate help in this kind of family crisis. That includes knowledge of the legal requirements and appropriate local contacts, as well as some basic insight into the situation itself. Prompt action can be essential in such circumstances, and it only makes things worse if something happens and the Church does not know what to do.

Working in Partnership

Problems in this area of human behaviour can only be tackled by the church in partnership with other agencies, especially when any form of illegal or criminal activity is involved. In the UK, these agencies would include the police as well as groups such as Women's Aid, local government social work departments, and a variety of voluntary child support organizations. Other Western countries have broadly similar provision. Churches that are serious about family well-being need to be in contact with groups like this in advance of actually needing to liaise with them. Christians often seem to imagine that secular agencies are not interested in working with religious groups. Our experience shows the exact opposite. Resources are never enough to handle family problems satisfactorily, and the more people who are prepared to make a contribution, the better. The problem is that Christians can give the impression that they have all the answers, and are intent on either correcting what they see as wrong approaches on the part of social workers, or assuming that the Church knows how to do it because Christians are not implicated in this kind of family dysfunction. Social workers know that is not true. Religious faith can actually be a complicating factor that makes healing for wounded families more difficult, not easier. Christians with slick answers and intransigent attitudes are unlikely to be of much help. There is no magic wand that can be waved to correct dysfunctional situations, and anyone who thinks there is understands nothing about human emotions and relationships. A Biblical Gospel does not offer a quick fix, but points to the possibility of resurrection after pain and suffering – calling those who are wounded to take up their cross and follow Jesus.

If we consciously follow the example and teaching of Jesus, we need never be ashamed of being Christians. Not only does Jesus provide us with many instructive models for lifting up those who are broken, but he also encourages the acceptance of all whose values match those of God's kingdom (Mark 9:38-41). In this context, that certainly includes social work and other statutory agencies. The Church should therefore approach these bodies as potential partners, who are also working in the same community, and who share a common concern for the well-being of the same group of people. Starting a dialogue can best be done by a key worker from the Church (not necessarily a clergy person) approaching the person in charge of the respective organizations.' It may take a bit longer to arrange a meeting with the person at the top, but doing so shows a seriousness of purpose. Don't imagine that a social worker who happens to be a member of the Church is likely to be the best person to do this. It is unwise to generalize, but quite often Christians who are social workers have a different personal agenda from the service as a whole, and can be held at arm's length by their colleagues for that reason. By going through that route you can end up being unhelpfully labelled before a dialogue has even begun. It will always be more effective for a church to approach social work through official channels, and then the relationship starts with a totally clean slate.

At a meeting, be more willing to listen than to talk, but never be afraid to mention that you are a Christian. There is a growing awareness of the importance of spirituality for the healing of broken relationships, and secular agencies often find themselves utilizing so-called 'New Age' therapies because no one else seems to have anything to offer. You could also exchange information about areas of interest you have in common, and the resource the Church can offer (people as well as buildings). This is the time to ask for the information that you would like to have available to support your own dealings with families – things like the number to call if someone discloses personal abuse, or the emergency number that can mobilize a team to attend episodes of violence at any time of day or night. Get to know how social work agencies and the police operate, and what the correct procedures are. Well-meaning amateurs can unwittingly make things more difficult for statutory agencies, and they will respect the fact that you want to follow the proper guidelines (many of which are, of course, legal requirements).

It can be worth a group from the Church meeting a group of local social workers. Try to learn what is involved in their job. Get a social worker to make a presentation giving you a run-down of a typical week's work. In reality, there is no such thing, because the job is totally unpredictable, but hearing what a particular week was like will give you an insight into that and an understanding of some of the pressures. Better still, ask if it is possible to shadow a social worker for a day, or even a few hours. Ask if there are any needs in the community which the local social work department is aware of and with which they feel the Church might be able to give some assistance. Don't expect an immediate outcome from a first meeting. Trust needs to be built up in order to establish the basis of a working relationship. This could lead to an exciting project. One church we know went down this route, and found itself as a partner in an advisory service which was jointly sponsored by the Church, the local government social services department, and a charity. At the very least, if you have a relationship with such bodies it will make an enormous difference when you are faced with a real-life crisis situation.

Violence against Women

Until the late 1960s, domestic violence and abuse was scarcely a known issue at all, and it was not until Erin Pizzey published her ground-breaking book *Scream Quietly or the Neighbours Will Hear* that it began to attract widespread public attention.[2] Now, there is a continuing increase in the number of reported cases of men battering their wives, inflicting serious injury and sometimes death. The

Church seems to have a problem in knowing how to engage with this, for several reasons. Theology is still a major influencing factor for many. They may not realize it, but Christians who base their understanding of marriage and the family on the submission of women to men are tacitly accepting that violence against women can be appropriate behaviour. It is an inevitable result that if submission is the theory, then violence will be an acceptable practice.[3]

In addition to this, however, there is a tendency in the Church to assume that violence is a problem only in society at large, but not in the Church. The reality is quite different. Christian families are no different from other families, and battered women come from all walks of life, regardless of class, ethnicity, or religious involvement. In research carried out in the mid-1980s, James and Phyllis Alsdurf found that 'for every sixty married women in a church, ten suffer emotional and verbal abuse, and two or three will be physically abused by their husbands'.[4] In interviews carried out as part of our own research for this book, clergy were asked how they would react to an incident of domestic violence involving members of their congregation. Almost all of them denied its existence. One minister of a small, somewhat economically oppressed village said that in the fifteen years he had ministered in that parish he had not come across one single incident in his congregation. He must have had his eyes and ears closed. If we were to list families known to us where domestic violence is or has been an issue, it would read like a roll call of household names in the Christian world.

Unless we are prepared to recognize this, then obviously we are unlikely to do much about it. Part of the difficulty is that churches are still largely male-dominated institutions, and their structures reflect a male mind-set and style of doing things. For male leaders, facing the issue of violence against women is not a pastoral problem that can be kept at arm's length: it is something that is a potential personal threat for every man in the Church. Our natural defence mechanisms are bound to play a part in ensuring that the subject is taken less seriously than it deserves.

At a meeting between leading women in the Scottish churches and workers with Women's Aid, it was reported that in a particular city

Women's Aid had taken an initiative to share information about their work with other civic bodies, and to invite them to work in partnership to address the question of domestic violence. They wrote to the police, statutory social work agencies, local government departments, schools, libraries, lawyers, doctors, community centres, and churches. The letter was not a circular, and was not sent out indiscriminately. In each case, the most appropriate contact person had been identified by name, and a letter specifically addressed to them. In the case of the churches, the effort had been made to find the name of each clergy person so they could be contacted individually (not a particularly easy task, as it also involved identifying several different denominations and then searching through the relevant directories and handbooks). Overall, the approach had met with a warm and positive response – but not one single church had even taken the bother to reply, let alone indicate a willingness to engage in partnership. Also, it seemed to make no difference whether the clergy were men or women (a surprising fact that also emerged in the course of our own research – along with the observation that a person's theological position also seems irrelevant).

Defining Violence

Violence can take many forms, of which physical injury is only one. Psychological and emotional violence can include the withdrawal of normal love and affection, as well as verbal abuse. In Christian homes, words are often used by men who, for a variety of reasons, avoid physical violence. Men who are good at preaching sermons are by definition skilled in the use of words, and can (and do) use them to great effect as a means of imposing control over their wives. For men who live in a world dominated by words and cognitive understanding, verbal violence can be just as satisfying as physical assault, and has the advantage of being invisible in a church community where bruising and other marks of physical violence would not easily go unnoticed. One of the most insidious aspects of domestic violence is the ease with which it does become invisible. Even when its existence is obvious, there is a built-in tendency for all concerned to close ranks and deny that anything is happening. The wife of a well-known evangelical Christian leader in the UK has been beaten up by her husband for years, but says she will never admit to it publicly because people would think she was an inadequate wife, and in any case no one would believe her husband could ever behave that way.

It is easy to be simplistic, and impossible to generalize, but there is no question that violence thrives most readily in homes where the family structure is already dysfunctional in some way. The patriarchal family, with its strict hierarchy of control and domination, is almost set up for this very purpose. For many Christian women this is precisely the problem. They feel that being obedient to their husbands is an intrinsic part of a Christian relationship, and that whatever their husbands do must in some way be right, or for their own good. If they are 'punished' by being beaten, they easily rationalize it as the result of some great sin in their lives – so, far from being resistant, they ought to accept such chastisement as being from God. Anyone who doubts that this kind of argument is still put forward at the end of the twentieth century should read some of the case studies reported in Joy Bussert's book *Battered Women*, which not only contains accounts written by violent men and their victims, but also gives examples of the kind of church teaching which leads to such attitudes. Among others, she quotes the opinion of Elizabeth Rye Hanford, that 'a woman must ignore her feelings about the will of God and do what her husband says. She is to obey her husband as if he were God himself. She can be as certain of God's will when her husband speaks as if God had spoken audibly from heaven.'[5]

In the light of teaching like that (and it does not date from the 1940s or 50s, but from the mid-1980s), it is obvious that domestic violence in the Church frequently has a theological dimension. Clergy who vacillate about such matters as 'submission' of wives to husbands will be unlikely to have much to contribute to the healing of families that are broken. Our research indicated that this is exactly the position in a majority of churches. Many church leaders – maybe most – regularly counsel women in violent and abusive situations to return to their husbands, either for the sake of keeping their marriage intact or for the sake of their children. Others offer simplistic solutions by suggesting that prayer is the answer, and if suffering women will only accept the situation and pray about it then things will somehow work out all right.

Helping the Victim

At several points in this book we have been quite negative about prevailing Christian attitudes. We make no apology for that, particularly in relation to patriarchal theology and church structures. But there are many church leaders who want to be more helpful. What can we now do? Part of the answer lies in what we have also repeatedly emphasized: the Church must be a genuine community of caring people, which will be seen as a refuge for those who are hurting, and an appropriate place to seek help for problems with battering and other forms of abuse. First and foremost, people need to feel confident in turning to the Church for comfort and healing. But there are also a number of specific things that we can do.[6]

As part of our general store of knowledge, we should know about the laws concerning domestic violence, and about the local facilities which offer advice and protection to women in this situation. It is too late to start finding out about such things when a case presents itself to us. We also need to promote general awareness of the issue within the congregation. This will include the need to re-examine the messages we communicate from the pulpit and in our Bible study groups. Do we sidestep things by making vague statements about authority within the family, which then leave people struggling with the questions we described through Clare and Martin's experience in chapter 5? We can also encourage the whole Christian community to be a place of hospitality and healing for the survivors of violence, and make special provision for the recognition of their predicament during services of reconciliation and healing. It is also helpful to have materials available that will highlight some of these issues. Though reading a book will never resolve a deep personal crisis, we should have suitable literature available for victims to take, or to be given to them when they come looking for help. Marie Fortune's small booklet *Keeping the Faith: Questions and Answers for the Abused Woman* is an outstanding resource for this purpose, though seems to be little used especially in Britain.[7]

We also need to be realistic about how violence is likely to come to our notice. Women will not often come to our church vestries and offices and announce that they are being assaulted by their husbands. More usually, they will present more general questions or problems. They need us to be sensitive and give them space to address the difficult matters that may be hidden beneath the surface. Battered women will not easily share any of this with a man. If men are the problem, then it stands to reason that they are not going to be the solution to it as well. Churches need to have readily accessible women on their staff, not just as supplementary workers, but as clergy. Even then, it is not easy for battered women to relate to church staff. Rita-Lou Clarke captures the dilemma exactly: 'If you are white and male, you will need to be especially aware of the gap between you and the battered woman in terms of world–view. You are a member of the dominant culture . . . If you are a female pastor, you may have trouble understanding the helplessness of some battered women, for you have made the system work for you to a greater degree [than they have].'[8]

It may seem elementary, but once the communication barrier has been broken it is crucial that we believe what we are told. If the person being accused is a Christian – especially a key worker or minister – it can challenge our preconceptions. But it is exceedingly rare for people to invent stories of violence and abuse. When that does happen it is almost always done by a person who is highly disturbed in some other obvious way. It is more usual for women to minimize the extent of their suffering, which means that no matter how horrific it seems, what we are being told is likely to be only a tiny fraction of the full story.

We also need to be ready to challenge the violence without backing down. Some violent men actually want to change their behaviour, and all they need is for a third party to challenge them to do so. But there are many more who will react by denying what is going on, and it is important not to do anything that might make the woman's situation worse. It is essential, first, because any confrontation with an offender can put his victim in even more danger. But secondly, women who are beaten have a very low self-esteem. They need to know that there is nothing more shameful about being battered than about being run over by a bus. They need to be lifted up and affirmed, and assured of their special value. That includes empowering them no longer to be pawns in someone else's game, but to take responsibility for themselves. Church workers should never act without a woman's consent. She must always be encouraged to take steps to protect herself and her children, but ultimately she will be the best judge of her own best interest. Remember, though, that people in crisis often need prompt action if their situation is not to deteriorate. Depending on the stage in the violence at which advice is sought, victims may be so confused and uncertain that this can be one of the few occasions when it is helpful to have another person take control of things. But that should always be on a short-term basis.

In the longer term, a victim of violence will need to assess the prospects for her continuing relationship with a man who consistently beats her up. Breaking up a relationship is never easy, even when it is dominated by negative experiences. Though Christians imagine people get divorced for trivial reasons, that is hardly ever the case. Commitment in relationships is unquestionably an important Christian value. But commitment works both ways, and involves mutual accountability. The marriage covenant is wrecked just as effectively through violence as it is through adultery.'

Clergy are sometimes inclined to suggest marriage counselling for couples locked in a cycle of repeated violence. But violence is not a marriage problem: it is a man's problem. The suggestion of marriage counselling immediately implies that both partners need to change. That can give a subtle message to the woman, that she is somehow to blame for what is happening – while it assures her husband that what he is doing is not so bad after all, and may even be excusable. There are also other reasons why marriage counselling should never be the first line of approach. The immediate goal must always be to stop the violence. Unless the violence is stopped (and that usually involves some form of treatment or therapy for the man), marriage counselling will be, at best, a waste of time, and at worst might even add to the violence, by giving the man yet more excuses to be displeased with his wife. In the meantime, whatever else happens, the woman needs a safe place to live, and help to rebuild her damaged sense of self-worth. She may not need to live on her own in the long term but until she knows she can, it will be an uphill struggle to reconstruct a new form of relationship with the same man.

The Cycle of Violence

Domestic violence operates in a complex and cyclical fashion. At those points in the cycle where violence is at its peak, the obvious solution might seem to be for the woman to leave the relationship. But it is not that simple, as there are also points in the cycle when everything seems fine – even perfect. A typical scenario runs like this.[10] Something happens to the man, and triggers the building of tension. It can be absolutely anything, from being angry with his boss, or not getting a promotion in his job, to getting chicken for dinner instead of steak. His wife will probably try very hard to do everything right so as not to annoy him more. But it seldom works, and the things she does to try and calm him down might even become (from his point of view) provocative actions.

It is only a matter of time before there is an emotional explosion – 'volcanic violence' it has been called.[11] Something happens (probably something trivial and unpredictable), things go over the edge, and violence breaks out. After that, of course, the violent husband is sorry. He enters what he wants to be a kind of honeymoon phase, promising that nothing like this will ever happen again, and pleading to be forgiven. He might even offer to seek professional help if he is accepted by his wife and given one more chance. Even if his wife is reluctant to believe him (and why should she?), he may still insist on making things up. For many men, the only way they know how to do this is by having sex, and when that happens the violence and exploitation can just move into another gear, and assault leads to rape. In due course the cycle will repeat itself. It might take another hour, or it could be another six months, or even longer. But unless this man really wants to change, and gets help to do so, things will go from bad to worse. Evidence shows that as time passes, violent men become less and less apologetic for their behaviour.

It is easy for clergy to advise women to forgive, but forgiveness must be balanced with a demand for repentance on the part of the violent man. Women do not need to forgive and forget: they need to forgive and remember. There will be no healing if the experience is forgotten. It needs to be worked through and put in proper perspective. This will almost always require specialist help for both parties. Ministers often like to call themselves 'professional' people. But we need to know what we are professional at, and recognize there are some situations in which we are not likely to be competent. In cases like this, there will often be legal questions that need to be handled, as well as the emotional issues.

The church should not expect to hand over all responsibility to other agencies, though. People need a safe space – psychological as well as physical – to help them find complete healing. Think of the woman mentioned in Luke 8:43-48. She had not been physically assaulted, but she was untouchable. No-one wanted to know her. She was victimised, and she felt ashamed. What did Jesus do for her? He noticed she was there, and accepted her as she was – and out of that she found healing. Maybe the one thing that Christians can do is to acknowledge people's suffering, instead of feeling uncomfortable about it.

Violent Offenders

Helping victims is one thing, dealing with the perpetrators of violence is quite a different matter. Where a criminal act has been committed, they might end up with a prison sentence. Christians, of all people, should realize that simply condemning someone who has done wrong is not particularly helpful. On the other hand, many violent offenders continue to deny their offence even if they are found guilty by a court. That is their way of handling what they have done. Rehabilitation is a long and complex business, requiring considerable commitment on the part of anyone who becomes involved.

But why do they do it anyway? Some of them are psychopaths, or suffer from other personality disorders. But not all of them fall into that category – not even the majority. Researchers working in the rehabilitation of violent men are concluding that a strong element of social conditioning is involved. It has long been recognized that violent men have often grown up in violent homes. But violence in men also seems to be related to wider cultural norms related to the understanding of what it means to be male or female. We saw in our very first chapter how closely our understandings of the family have followed the philosophical ideals of Western culture. Part of that has been the consistent expectation that, to be a real man at all is to be in control – a belief that, in the Christian context, has often been backed up by a selective and culturally-conditioned approach to Scripture.[12] Being in control not only manifests itself as a need to be the boss, but to be in control of oneself, particularly the emotions. The 'stiff upper lip' of Western (especially British) men is legendary. Showing emotion, we have been told, is for cissies. To put it another way, men are often conditioned to deny what might be described as the feminine side of their nature. All their education focuses on developing cognitive skills. As a result, they can be highly trained surgeons, lawyers, teachers, or whatever, while having no skills at all in the emotional side of their lives.

In our culture at large, we have elevated the rational and down-graded the emotional. We have worshipped what is individual and despised what is relational. As a result, men cannot express feelings, and may even be unaware of their existence. In so far as they know how to feel, only two emotional routes are open to them: happiness or anger. In this frame of reference, more subtle negative emotions such as sadness, disappointment, or a sense of vulnerability only have one possible outlet: anger. Joy Bussert concludes that 'The emotional damage done to men in our culture through this depri-vation of feelings is . . . at the heart of the problem of violence in the home . . . *battering – at least in part – is a substitute for tears* . . .'.[13] This also helps to explain why at the same time as they crave to be dominant, violent men are often profoundly dependent on their wives.[14] It is also the reason why throughout this book we have laid so much emphasis on the need for the church to take a positive lead in active support of families, particularly by modelling a Christian understanding of community. Whole people do not produce dysfunctional families. Healing of the emotions, and the discovery by both women and men of what it means to be made in the image of God, will be at the heart of a truly Christian understanding of the family. It is much easier to help men find their new identity through Christ than it is to help them escape the cycle of domestic violence once they have gone down that road.

Abuse of Children

Violence and abuse are but two sides of the same coin. Indeed, depending on how the words are used and defined, they can easily be referring to the same things.[15] Any generalization is open to misinterpretation, but homes in which men attack their partners tend on the whole also to be homes in which children are more at risk. Much of what we have already said about violence against women will also apply to situations involving children. The underlying causes, both social and psychological, are often very similar.[16] But it is not just men who abuse children, and it is not only parents: it can be, and often is, other close relatives or people living in and about the same house. That makes children especially vulnerable, because they cannot necessarily count on any adult in their family taking their side. If, as sometimes happens, their mother seems to support them against their father one day, then she can be just as likely to be the one to abuse them the next. Moreover, their size and relative physical weakness puts them at a disadvantage in any dealings with adults.

Varieties of Abuse

Children can suffer in many ways, but there are several identifiable forms of abuse that are the most common.

Physical assault includes any non-accidental injury, from slapping to murder. Its causes are broadly similar to the factors that lead men to be violent against women, and relate to the perceived need of parents to be in control of the family situation. Because of the way it is often linked to beliefs about discipline, it requires some careful handling in the pastoral situation.[17] Within society as a whole different attitudes can be found, and what to one group might look like a harmful form of discipline might be perfectly normal to another. But there are some general parameters to provide guidance. Everyone accepts that anything resulting in physical injury (bruises, cuts, broken bones) is unacceptable. A variation on physical assault of the child can be the wanton destruction of property or pets that are important to the child. This can be just as hurtful as being beaten. Indeed, it is sometimes used as a form of discipline by parents for that very reason.

Psychological or emotional abuse is also common. A child is threatened with the withholding of love and affection or is constantly teased or degraded in some way. A child may be constantly criticized in front of her friends, or other siblings. Her clothes are never as tidy as someone else's, her hair is not properly combed, she never says the right thing, and so on. This kind of abuse is widespread, especially among Christian families. A survey conducted in 12,000 evangelical Christian homes came to the conclusion that 'although many Christian families are not marked by physical violence, many do experience emotional abuse'.[18] This can take many forms. In addition to those already mentioned, it includes religious abuse, for example by threatening a child with Bible verses that seem to condemn his or her behaviour, or making God's acceptance of them dependent on certain forms of permissible behaviour.[19] It can also involve repressing their emotions ('I don't want any crying') – something that, if our overall understanding of domestic dysfunction is correct, can have catastrophic consequences for future generations of families as well as the individuals concerned. Calling a child names, and manipulating them to do what parents want, or refusing to speak at all until they conform, are all techniques in the armoury of parents who use emotional blackmail to control their offspring. Another variation occurs when parents try to work out their own unfulfilled ambitions through their children. From an early age, Olive was told that she was destined to become a missionary. Her mother had herself been inspired by tales of Victorian adventurers, and regretted she never had the chance to be one herself. The next best thing was to live it out through the next generation, especially through a child whose birth could be made to appear the reason why the parent's own dream had never come to pass. In the long term, of course, manipulation rarely achieves what it is intended to do. Instead, it leads to a breakdown of relationships between children and parents, and stores up problems for the future if the child in adult life then tries to manipulate other people.

Neglect is another form of child abuse. Here again, expectations can vary from one cultural group to another, and what seems reasonable in one context may be thought harsh somewhere else. For some, depriving a child of food for a day may be seen as brutal. Others might have the same opinion of parents who expect a child of five to sleep in a room alone at night. But neglect can generally be defined as the lack of provision of basic needs of food, clothing and shelter. It can also include circumstances in which a young child is expected to take responsibility for other family members. The misuse of alcohol is often a factor here.

Sexual abuse covers many different things, including incest, rape, having intercourse with children, taking indecent photographs of them, encouraging them to become prostitutes, and a collection of other practices generally subsumed under the terminology of 'lewd and libidinous behaviour'. However, defining the phenomenon is the easy part: proving that something has taken place, and if so what, is by no means straightforward. Though it is always against the law, there is considerable debate among the professionals about what constitutes appropriate proof of sexual abuse, especially when it involves sexual intercourse of one sort or another.

All these forms of abuse are similar, especially in terms of their pastoral consequences.[20] Sexual abuse, for example, has a close relationship with violence, both in its causes and manifestations. It is impossible to predict in advance which children are going to be most at risk from which types of abuse. Abusive parents do not always abuse all their children. Sometimes one child is singled out as especially disruptive or difficult, and once the cycle is established, then both parents and child take it for granted that the child is the problem.

Recognizing Abuse

It is easy to give checklists of the signs of possible abuse, and many books on the subject do so. There is no doubt that a child's behaviour can reveal a lot about what is going on. When behavioural patterns change without any other obvious reason, it will be natural for the sensitive counsellor to look for some other, perhaps hidden, explanation. Some children who are being abused in the home become shy and introverted, while others become hyperactive. Some become aggressive and angry, while others become very domesticated, as if they are trying to take the home over and correct things so as to compensate for the immaturity of the actual parents. Many develop problems with sleeping, wetting the bed unexpectedly or having constant nightmares. Abuse can lead to the development of eating disorders. Other children become chronically withdrawn, depressed, submissive and fearful. They are reluctant to go to certain places, which can sometimes include home (many kids who wander about the streets do so because that seems to be safer than going home). School work might also suffer. History or mathematics seem less important when your whole life is being turned upside down. Some therapists have developed more specific indicators. For example, it has been claimed that a child who is sexually abused will tend to draw people with no hands or feet. Others point out that an abused child can find it difficult to walk alongside an adult, preferring instead to walk behind in a submissive posture. It is possible to make too much out of such things. There is no one set of behavioural signs that necessarily indicate a child is being abused, nor is the presence of one or more of these necessarily a sign of abuse. Perhaps the one exception is when children make sexual advances to other children. Children who show evidence of explicit sexual knowledge, and who are prepared to act out what they know, are almost certainly victims of sexual abuse.

It is more common for those who work a lot with children to develop a general feeling of unease. Olive recalls an incident in Jamaica as she was leaving a church with a group of clergy. As they walked down the street, the group passed a child who just looked very sad. No one gave her a second glance, except Olive and one other person. They both had extensive experience of abused children, and though only one of them was in their own cultural context there was something about the child's body language that instinctively caused them both to ask the same questions. There is a degree of perception which comes from experience. When working with a group of children on a regular basis, it is even easier to pick up the hidden signals that something may be wrong. Churches which run activities for children with different teams of people alternating with one another are at a disadvantage here. If adults are to be accessible and user-friendly to children, continuity is important. Church people who are involved with children and young people ought to be given training to help them recognize different behavioural patterns, and have some minimal understanding of the problems of abuse. It is neither possible nor desirable for every children's worker to become a psychoanalyst (and well-meaning amateurs can do more harm than good), but some basic training on this subject, combined with an understanding of stages of faith development could revolutionize our entire approach to youth work and children's ministry.[21]

Helping Victims

As with any personal crisis, effective pastoral support begins with an adequate understanding of the problem, and its likely effects on the victim. One thing is absolutely certain in relation to child abuse: children are never responsible for abuse which happens to them.

If a child reveals a situation of abuse to an adult, it is important first of all to believe them and take their story seriously. Exactly the same thing is true here as with women who are victims of violence: there will be a tendency to under-report, rather than exaggerate. In the case of disclosure of sexual abuse, adult society has had an inbuilt tendency to play it down. This goes back to the dominant influence of the theories of Sigmund Freud about women's sexual fantasies. In his own clinical experience, he discovered that women were repeatedly reporting cases of sexual abuse at the hands of their fathers. In the face of all the facts (maybe because he was unable to handle them personally), he eventually concluded that this was a result of their own wishful thinking, and thereby laid a bogus scientific foundation for the reticence of society at large to give credence to such claims.[22] However, we now know differently. Allegations of sexual abuse must be taken seriously. Children who are being actively abused find it hard to share this experience with other people. For one thing, the abuser is always likely to be in a position of authority over them, and may offer bribes or threats to prevent them reporting what is taking place. In addition, the child may secretly believe it is his or her fault anyway, and be afraid of being accused of doing something wrong. Moreover, children naturally fear that if they tell their story the whole family will fall apart – and it will be their fault. The abuser may already have warned the child of this possibility. Some might even be enjoying the special attention they are receiving, even though it is also painful and confusing. If a child does disclose sexual abuse, therefore, it is extremely important to reassure her that she has done the right thing, and for an adult to act with absolute integrity that will not betray their trust. If the parents are implicated, this means not going straight to them to report what has been disclosed. Too often, children have reported things to adults who have not only not believed them, but have then informed the very adults who are abusing them. In any case of alleged sexual abuse, it is essential that the appropriate authorities are informed, and that this is done quickly, especially if the abuser is resident in the same house as the victim. Abuse is not just a moral aberration: it is a crime. But if swift action is not taken, the family will close ranks and deny that anything has taken place. At the same time, the victim is likely to be at even greater risk for having let the family secret slip out. Incidentally, while it is true that most victims of sexual abuse are girls, there is an increasing trend for boys to be victims, quite often at the hands of female relatives (particularly an aunt or even a mother).[23]

Once a case has been disclosed, what happens next will vary from one jurisdiction to another. In cases of incestuous sexual abuse it is likely to include the removal of either child or abuser from the home, at least on a temporary basis until the situation can be properly assessed. When this happens, it can present the child with a dilemma. If she is the one to be removed, she may feel punished and conclude that she was in the wrong anyway. Either way, she is likely to feel regret at having broken up the family. She may also be the recipient of aggression from the non-offending parent (who will not necessarily know what has been going on). Support for the child and for this parent will be crucial, because their relationship is the one that is most likely to survive on a long-term basis. In this context, the kind of support the Church can most usefully give is simply by being there and being available. Specialist counselling needs to be left to those who are equipped for that.

In terms of the development of a child's faith and value-system, abuse of all kinds has profound and far-reaching destructive consequences. We referred in an earlier chapter to the researches of Christian educators such as John Westerhoff, and the conclusion that a child's faith in God is facilitated by relationships with parents. The parental rejection that is involved in child abuse is always damaging, and has wide-ranging repercussions. Disturbed children become disturbed adults. Children who experience nothing but anger and violence from their parents develop a distorted image of God, which in later life typically leads them to give up on faith altogether. 'Because they were betrayed by those they trusted most, victims of abuse have trouble trusting anyone, including God.'[24] They also develop a perverted understanding of love, and the relationship between suffering and joy. Abused children are receiving conflicting messages from their parents: 'they love me, they hurt me, therefore love is the same thing as pain'. Unless this deviant logic is corrected by future experiences of unconditional love and acceptance, they may go on as adults to inflict the same suffering on others, often without any conscious realization of what they are doing, or that this is abnormal behaviour.

Helping Parents

Appropriate ways of helping parents will depend on whether the child abuse has taken place in the family, or outside. It will be a good deal easier to help those whose child has been abused by a stranger. They will feel it as keenly as if they had been abused themselves. The good news is that 'Children living in homes with secure and re-assuring parents who experience sexual abuse by a stranger show little lasting effects.'[25] Still, that can be hard to handle when you're in the midst of the crisis. The parents are also victims, and just like the child they will need a lot of reassurance. This time, they will need to know that they are good parents, and they really can care for their children. It was not their fault if a stranger abducted their child in the street, or a neighbour or a friend's father abused them. It may be, though, that there will be an element of truth in some of the things they feel. Perhaps their schedule is too busy, and they spend too much time at work without making adequate provision for their children to be cared for. In that case, they need help to work out how to change things and revise their priorities. This will include helping them to identify appropriate boundaries for the child that will be fair. For example, there will be an understandable temptation to restrict the child's movements, so that he or she is not so vulner-able. Adults can see that the child might be safer staying at home, but for a child that can look like punishment, as if they were to blame for what happened all along. There will also be unfinished business to work through with the abuser – and with God. These are things that only the couple concerned can address, which is why reflective listening will be of more help than much speaking. In due course, questions like this might usefully be aired in the context of a support group with other parents.

Helping parents who are themselves implicated in abusive

situations is a lot more difficult. We have already said a little about support for the non-offending parent. Helping the offender will be a tougher business. For a start, he is likely to be subject to some legal restrictions, and may be physically removed to prison. On top of that, he is unlikely to be prepared to face up to what he has done. Incidentally, if a man comes to you to confess to sexual abuse, don't be hoodwinked into treating it lightly. He is probably looking for a quick dispensation of forgiveness, and hoping to avoid the messy consequences of his actions that way. The reality is that sex offenders are devious people. Almost all of them have some fundamental psychological flaw, that on the one hand allows them to be very authoritarian people with a strict moral code, while at the same time exploiting their own – or other people's – vulnerable children. Don't be tempted to have too much sympathy for them. The facts you need to remember are:

- Sex offenders rarely tell the truth. They deny what has happened, or do their best to minimize it. They hardly ever accept the full reality of what they have done.

- They very rarely express any regret for what they have done, or any sense that it was not right.

- They will always try to squirm out of accepting the consequences of their actions. In practical terms, that means they are likely to try to talk church leaders into providing them with a character reference, or telling a court that, even if they did it, it was so out of character that they should be given a second chance.

- Sexual abuse is addictive: once an offender starts, it is difficult to stop. Compulsory enrolment in a treatment programme may or may not work, but more often than not the intervention of the law is the only way to stop them.

Anyone who tries to minister to sex offenders needs to be realistic about the chances of rehabilitation, and under no circumstances appear to condone or even excuse what has happened. Offering support to an offender will be a long-term business, and should always be in conjunction with a recognized rehabilitation programme. Never be tempted to become the front-line provider of primary care.[26]

Abusive Families

Prevention is always better than cure, and the provision of adequate support for families can play a significant part in avoiding the destructive kind of dysfunction we have examined in this chapter. There is a general consensus that abusive families share many of the same characteristics. Like all checklists, this one is a generalization, but identifying some of the features of a family at risk can be a major help in alerting the sensitive Christian to a pastoral need.

Recognizing the Signs

Abusive parents have experienced abusive behaviour themselves. We all learn how to be parents by watching our own parents, and unless we take specific steps to learn different parenting skills we are likely to repeat all their mistakes. This includes sexual abuse, for it is widely believed that most abusers were themselves abused as children (though the reverse is not true, for not everyone who has been abused goes on to abuse other people).[27]

Abusive parents typically do not understand children's needs, and lack parenting skills. They are constantly comparing themselves unfavourably with other parents, whom they imagine are doing a better job, or are better informed. As a result of these perceived inadequacies, they feel guilty and inferior, and take it out on their children. They are probably harsh disciplinarians as well, because they know nothing at all about child development. They think of children not as little people, but as little adults, and imagine that children act in the same way and for the same reasons as adults would. Within the Christian community, this outlook may be complicated by the addition of a theological understanding of salvation couched exclusively in terms of an adult experience. In this context, children may be burdened with adult notions of sin and guilt that can adversely affect their own personal development.

Abusive families are also often isolated from neighbours and their own relatives. Friendships are discouraged, sometimes for moral or religious reasons (the parents don't want their children to mix with people with different opinions or lifestyles, which then become not just different but sinful). This in turn creates the impression that their family is special, and probably better than other families. When child abuse is introduced into this equation, the abusive behaviour then reinforces the feeling of difference from other families, and strengthens the pressures to be secretive about it and to stay isolated from the rest of society.

Abusing families can also find it difficult to allow their members much independence. The natural human desire for warm personal relationships is intensified to the point where the family becomes an end in itself. Parents with emotional problems inherited from their own childhood are hungry for love and acceptance, and compete with one another to see who can get the most. The one who loses out then turns to the children, but since they can never satisfy their needs they in turn become the objects of aggression.

Addressing the Problem

Finally, abusive families struggle to accept change. In this, they only reflect where our culture as a whole finds itself. Christians need to be prepared to draw attention to some of the inherent contradictions which we seem happy to live with. Although child sexual abuse is legally and morally forbidden in most cultures, the very same social and religious structures that frown on it also give implicit approval to hierarchies of power in which the child has no voice. Ultimately, our inability to handle abuse and domestic violence can be traced back to our inadequate social understandings of the family, in particular the attitude that sees women and children as mere adjuncts to men, if not actually the possessions of men. This sense of powerlessness and secrecy contributes to the damage which is caused to victims, and which they carry with them through the rest of their life. One of the ironic things about sexual abuse is that it is not mainly about sexual acts, but about the distortion of relationships, the betrayal of trust and the abuse of power. The practical problems will not begin to be resolved until we address some fundamental issues about power within the family.

But there are also specific practical things that churches can do. Churches are not the only organizations that can provide support for families in crisis, and we have already emphasized the importance of partnership with other agencies. But the spiritual dimension of the healing of broken relationships is important, and should be a significant component of what the church has to offer. Support groups are so valuable precisely because of this, as they provide a chance for people to move on from receiving help to giving it to others. The longer you are in a group the more you see yourself changing from being the person who needs all the assistance to the one who starts to support others. That discovery alone can work wonders for a person's self-image.

Providing opportunity for prayer is also important. Until we can work through the difficult experiences we cannot know complete healing. The sacraments have a special part to play at this point. The words of a liturgy can be especially helpful at a time when our own words are inadequate to match our feelings. We have said a lot here about the value of groups, but there are many times when people need to be alone. It can be worth creating a suitable space within the church building, a small room or side chapel, or just a corner where people can retreat and be quiet, or ask for prayer. Some physical thing to give expression to unspoken – and unspeakable – emotions can be helpful, such as the possibility of lighting a candle or drawing something on a sheet of paper or in a book. Sharing the Eucharist with other Christians also opens us up to being able to receive and to express feeling again. Those in the Reformed tradition may need to ponder how they can incorporate things like anointing and confession/absolution in their pastoral ministry with people who are abused and distressed. This can be particularly helpful in situations where whole families are trying to restructure their lives following some disruptive episode. People scar one another to such an extent that it can take some time before it is possible for them to live together again. But we never move on by burying the past, and the one thing the Gospel does give us is a way to repent and experience forgiveness and also discover a capacity to forgive other people.

NOTES

1. Family History

1. For an accessible volume on the way the family has been portrayed in literature down through the ages, see Nicholas Tavuchis & William J Goode, *The Family Through Literature* (New York: McGraw Hill, 1975).

2. See, for example, Bert N. Adams, *The Family: a Sociological Interpretation* (Chicago: Rand McNally, 1975); Graham Allan, *Family Life* (Oxford: Blackwell, 1985); Mary Farmer, *The Family* (London: Longmans, 1970); Diana Gittins, *The Family in Question* (London: Macmillan, 1993 2nd ed); B. Gottlieb, *The Family in the Western World* (New York: OUP, 1993); C. C. Harris, *The Family: an Introduction* (London: Allen & Unwin, 1969); Barrie Thorne & Marilyn Yaloms (eds), *Rethinking the Family* (London: Longman, 1982); Adrian Wilson, *Family* (London: Tavistock, 1985); Robert F. Winch, *The Modern Family* (New York: Rinehart & Winston, 1971). On the family in different cultures, see Ruth Nanda Anshen, *The Family: its Function and Destiny* (New York: Harper & Row, 1959). And from a Christian perspective, Jack O. Balswick & Judith K. Balswick, *The Family* (Grand Rapids: Baker, 1991); Rodney Clapp, *Families at the Crossroads* (Downers Grove: InterVarsity, 1993).

3. Reported in the *Chicago Tribune*, May 25 1916.

4. *The Family in Question*, 60-72.

5. On the history of the family in many different cultures, the most comprehensive work is still Willystine Goodsell, *A History of Marriage and the Family* (New York: Macmillan, 1934); see also James Casey, *The History of the Family* (Oxford: Blackwell, 1989). James Wallace Milden, *The Family in Past Time* (New York: Garland, 1977) provides invaluable bibliographical guidance covering many historical periods.

6. It is quite beyond the scope of this work to give any sort of account of the Enlightenment and its impact on Western culture. For extensive discussion of its effects from a Christian standpoint, see Lesslie Newbigin's two books, *Foolishness to the Greeks* (Geneva: WCC, 1986); and *The Gospel in a Pluralist Society* (London: SPCK, 1989). On the cultural context as it affects Christian witness and worldview, see John Drane, 'Salvation and Cultural Change', in *Windows on Salvation*, ed Donald English (London: Darton, Longman & Todd, 1994), 166-80.

7. Edward Goldsmith, *The Way: An Ecological World-View* (London, 1992), 171. Our emphasis.

8. Awareness of the human rights issues surrounding the patriarchal exploitation of women goes back further than that, at least to the eighteenth century. Mary Wollstonecraft wrote her *Vindication of the Rights of Women* as early as 1792, while William Thompson's *Appeal of One Half of the Human Race against the Pretensions of the Other Half* (1825) and John Stuart Mill's *On the Subjection of Women* (1869) were also influential. The UK government's *Married Women's Property Act* (1882) began the process of legislative change, though there was still a long way to go after that.

9. On the changes taking place in the nature of work see, most accessibly, Charles Handy's two works, *The Age of Unreason* (London: Business Books, 1989), especially 137-402; and *The Empty Raincoat* (London: Hutchinson, 1994).

10. Douglas Coupland, *Life After God* (London: Simon & Schuster, 1994). Coupland is also author of the influential *Generation X*, which documents in a novelistic way the search for meaningful community of today's younger generations.

2. Who are Today's Families?

1. Not everyone accepts that we ought to be redefining the family at all. For a defence of the view that we need a return to a normative understanding of family life, see J. Davies (ed.), *The Family: Is It Just Another Lifestyle Choice?* (London: IEA Health & Welfare Unit, 1993). This opinion is essentially motivated by reactionary political considerations, and from the point of view of pastoral ministry it represents a head-in-the-sand attitude that, far from advancing the church's mission, has the potential to inflict serious damage on the church's ability to communicate the Gospel effectively in contemporary culture.

2. For some of these, see R. N. Rapoport, M. P. Fogarty & R. Rapoport (eds), *Families in Britain* (London: Routledge & Kegan Paul, 1982), 121-354; Gwen B. Carr, *Marriage and Family in a Decade of Change* (Reading MA: Addison Wesley, 1977).

3. This is not the only reason why people take up full-time paid employment, of course. Other considerations would include the need to establish social contacts outside the home; the need to escape the potential boredom, frustration, loneliness and (for some) depression of domesticity; a desire to establish a personal independent identity that is not defined by reference to either marriage or parenthood; and the desire to practice and improve a worthwhile skill already acquired. But for a majority of people, the economic factor would be decisive.

4. For first-hand accounts of some of the difficulties facing those who are trying to blend families together, see Frank F. Furstenberg & Graham B. Spanier, *Recycling the Family: Remarriage after Divorce* (Beverly Hills CA: Sage, 1984); Brenda Maddox, *The Half-Parent: Living with Other People's Children* (London: Andre Deutsch, 1975). For a Christian perspective, see Laura Sherman Walters, *There's a New Family in My House* (Wheaton IL: Harold Shaw Publishers, 1993).

5. Ten-to-fourteen-year-olds are especially problematic in this respect: cf. the survey of research in M. Ambert & M. Baker, 'Marriage Dissolution', in B. Fox, *Family Bonds and Gender Division*

(Toronto: Canadian Scholars Press, 1988), 453-75.

6. Patricia Morgan, *Farewell to the Family? Public Policy and Family Breakdown in Britain and the USA* (London: Institute of Economic Affairs, 1995).

7. For a recent analysis of the possible outcomes of gay parenting, see A. E. Gottfried & A. W. Gottfried, *Redefining Families* (New York: Plenum, 1994), 131-70.

8. On custodial grandparenting, see A. E. Gottfried & A. W. Gottfried, *op. cit.* 171-220.

3. Being a Child in the Modern Family

1. Cf. S. Brody & S. Axelrod, *Mothers, Fathers & Children* (New York: International University Press, 1978).

2. For a succinct account of the impact of poverty on British families, cf. Harriett Wilson, 'Families in Poverty', in R. N. Rapoport, M. P. Fogarty & R. Rapoport, *Families in Britain*, 252-62.

3. Cf. S. McLanahan & L. Bumpass, 'Intergenerational consequences of family disruption', in *American Journal of Sociology* 94/1 (1988), 130-52.

4. Even otherwise sensitive thinkers can sometimes understand divorce as an exclusively adult concern: cf. the article by Jack Dominian, 'Families in Divorce' (in R. N. Rapoport, M. P. Fogarty & R. Rapoport, *Families in Britain*, 263-85) which, despite its title, makes no mention of the child's viewpoint on the matter.

5. For children's own stories of the way divorce impacted their lives, see Jill Krementz, *How it Feels when Parents Divorce* (London: Victor Gollancz, 1985); also Yvette Walczak, *Divorce: the Child's Point of View* (London: Harper & Row, 1984).

6. For discussions of child sexual abuse from a Christian perspective, cf. Florence Rush, *The Best Kept Secret: Sexual Abuse of Children* (New York: McGraw-Hill, 1980); Mary D. Pellauer, Barbara Chester & Jane A. Boyaiian (eds), *Sexual Assault and Abuse:*

A Handbook for Clergy and Religious Professionals (San Francisco: Harper & Row, 1987), 5-9, 172-97.

7. For more on 'religious abuse', see Wesley R. Monfalcone, *Coping with Abuse in the Family* (Philadelphia: Westminster Press, 1980), 45-57.

8. Cf. Diana Gittins, *The Family in Question*, 169-82.

9. In many respects nothing much has changed with regard to some of the root causes of sexual abuse in particular. Cf. the work by Anthony S. Wohl on incest in Victorian families, which identifies bad housing, cramped conditions, and social inequalities as major contributing factors (ch. 10 in Anthony S. Wohl, ed., *The Victorian Family*, London: Croom Helm, 1978).

10. For an outstanding treatment of the whole question of ministering to children in today's families, see Andrew D. Lester (ed), *When Children Suffer: A Sourcebook for Ministry with Children in Crisis* (Philadelphia: Westminster Press, 1987).

4. Being an Adult in Today's Family

1. Some (male) researchers are more optimistic about the extent to which home responsibilities are actually shared: cf. Robert O. Blood & Robert L. Hamblin, 'The Effects of the Wife's Employment on the Family', in N. W. Bell & E. F. Vogel, *A Modern Introduction to the Family* (New York: Free Press, 1968), 182-7. But anecdotal evidence from women virtually never supports such claims. Cf. also Graham Allen, *Family Life*, 25-52; and the wide-ranging discussion in T. Savells & L. J. Cross (eds), *The Changing Family*, 254-79. For some interesting case studies of good practice in the way different responsibilities may be juggled, cf. M. Hill *Sharing Child Care in Early Parenthood* (London: Routledge Kegan Paul, 1987).

2. Charles Handy, *The Empty Raincoat*, 178ff.

3. *Op.cit.*, 232.

4. According to Erik Erikson, this is related to the different ways in which men and women conceptualize space: cf. his essay, 'Inner

and Outer Space: Reflections on Womanhood', in N. W. Bell & E. F. Vogel, *A Modern Introduction to the Family*, 442-63.

5. Cf. C. Safilios-Rothschild, 'The study of family power structure: a review', in *Journal of Marriage and the Family* 32 (1970), 539-52; G. McDonald, 'Family Power: the assessment of a decade of theory and research, 1970-1979', in *Journal of Marriage and the Family* 42 (1980), 841-54; M. Szinovacz, 'Family Power', in M. Sussman & S. Steinmetz (eds), *Handbook of Marriage and the Family* (New York: Plenum, 1987), 651-93.

6. For a lot of men, of course, this is precisely the problem. Cf. William J. Goode, 'Why Men Resist', in B. Thorne & M. Yalom, *Rethinking the Family: Some Feminist Questions* (New York: Longman, 1982), 131-47.

7. Robert Bly, *Iron John: a Book about Men* (Shaftesbury: Element Books 1991). For an outstanding account of the predicament of men in different cultures today, cf. Errol Miller, *Men at Risk* (Kingston: Jamaica Publishing House, 1991). Most Christian books on the subject do not really get to grips with the new social reality at all, but see James Nelson, *The Intimate Connection: Male Sexuality, Masculine Spirituality* (Philadelphia: Westminster Press, 1988); Jack O. Balswick, *Men at the Crossroads* (Downers Grove: InterVarsity, 1992).

5. Bible Families

1. See Susan Brooks Thistlethwaite, 'Every Two Minutes: Battered Women and Feminist Interpretation', in L. M. Russell (ed.), *Feminist Interpretation of the Bible* (Philadelphia: Westminster Press, 1985), 96-107. Also the extensive documentation of the social consequences of this teaching in Joy M. K. Bussert, *Battered Women* (Minneapolis: Division for Mission of the Lutheran Church in America, 1986).

2. Christians have consistently made this mistake throughout the last 200-300 years, as one aspect of their faith after another has been accommodated to the prevailing ideologies of the European

Enlightenment – generally with disastrous consequences. On the essentially secular and (we would argue) non-Christian roots of hierarchical understandings of the family, see R. Emerson Dobash & Russell Dobash, *Violence Against Wives: A Case against the Patriarchy* (New York: The Free Press, 1979).

3. Wesley went so far as to make a virtue out of necessity, by claiming that if he had been a good husband and father he would have been a much less effective evangelist! See Stanley Ayling, *John Wesley* (London: Collins, 1979), 215-31; Henry D. Rack, *Reasonable Enthusiast* (London: Epworth, 1989), 251-69. On Livingstone, see Tim Jeal, *Livingstone* (London: Heinemann, 1973), 60-2, 110-2, 251.

4. Paul was certainly single at the time he wrote his letters, and even a cautious critic like F. F. Bruce believed this came about through divorce rather than the death of his spouse or never having been married: cf. his *Paul Apostle of the Free Spirit* (Exeter: Paternoster Press, 1977), 269-70.

5. For one of the few major works to address family change in the light of the Bible and its teaching, see Stephen B. Clark, *Man and Woman in Christ* (Ann Arbor: Servant Books, 1980).

6. For a survey and summary of some of the theological issues arising out of the way we use the Bible, see Rita-Lou Clarke, *Pastoral Care of Battered Women* (Philadelphia: Westminster Press, 1986), 61-85.

7. For a more extensive analysis of the Abraham story from the perspective of members of his family, and a discussion of the hermeneutical issues involved in doing so, see John Drane, *Evangelism for a New Age* (London: Marshall Pickering, 1994), 30-57.

8. There are some stories in the Old Testament which show women as having a certain amount of independence (people like Deborah, Esther, and some prophetesses). But in spite of this, they did not as a whole hold positions in government, or become priests. The family was always patriarchal in structure, and after the exile this became even more rigid as its assumptions were hardened into a very strict system of segregation between women and men.

9. For the rabbis' views on women's place, see the survey in O. L. Yarbrough, *Not Like the Gentiles* (Atlanta: Scholars Press, 1985), esp. 21-3.

10. For Rabbi Shammai, this could only mean a serious moral lapse such as adultery, whereas Rabbi Hillel argued divorce was justified for things as trivial as burning a meal. Mark and Matthew preserve different versions of Jesus' teaching (Mark 10:2-12, Matthew 19:1-12), but the key thing is that in both of them Jesus categorically rejected the notion that a man could divorce his wife on a whim. Jesus' teaching on divorce often causes concern to people who find themselves caught up in situations of breakdown, and has even been used as the justification for a total ban of divorce within the Christian community (see, for example, Andrew Cornes, *Divorce & Remarriage*, London: Hodder & Stoughton, 1993). A full discussion of this is not appropriate here, though it is worth noticing (i) that the early church always understood Jesus' statements on divorce as a starting point for decision-making, rather than absolute statements. They were regarded as signposts rather than detailed maps, and the diversity of New Testament statements on the subject confirms that: how otherwise could the early church have preserved the differences between Matthew (divorce for moral reasons) and Mark (no divorce)? To ask which is the original is to miss the point. (ii) In any case, Jesus regularly used deliberate exaggeration in order to make a point. In the very same chapter of Mark, when talking of riches and discipleship, he instructed his questioner to 'sell all your goods and give to the poor'. Elsewhere in the context of a saying on adultery, he recommended disciples to pull eyes out and cut hands off (Matthew 5:27-32). He could also speak of leaving father and mother in order to follow him (Mark 3:31ff). No one has ever imagined that these injunctions were to be followed to the letter: they have always been recognized as an engaging and compelling way to make a serious point. The fact that some want to apply Jesus' sayings on divorce literally, when from a literary point of view they fit the same model of rhetorical

exaggeration, says more about their own entrenched patriarchal attitudes than it does on the teaching of Jesus. For a survey of different exegetical opinions, and their impact on the pastoral task, see Cyril J. Barber, 'Marriage, Divorce and Remarriage', in *Journal of Psychology and Theology* 12 (1984), 170-7.

11. For example, only boys could read in the synagogue, while women and young children were confined to segregated sections.

12. Thistlethwaite, *op. cit.*, 102. Similarly, in John 4, Jesus had no hesitation accepting a woman who was caught up in situations of domestic tension, and affirming her worth, while at the same time inviting her to discipleship. This ability to lift up those who are broken, while challenging them to follow Jesus, is something modern Christians find very hard to emulate. On John 4, see more extensively John Drane, *Evangelism for a New Age*, 181-98.

13. For a summary presentation of all this, see John Drane, *Introducing the New Testament* (Oxford: Lion, 1986), 386-9.

14. Elizabeth Schussler Fiorenza suggests that Paul was consciously incorporating the teaching of Jesus about loving one's neighbour as oneself (Mark 12:31), see *In Memory of Her* (New York: Crossroad, 1983), 266-70. For a different interpretation of the passage, see Rosemary Radford Ruether, *Sexism and God-Talk* (Boston: Beacon, 1983), 141-2.

15. A conclusion backed up by Ernest Best's study *Paul and His Converts* (Edinburgh: T. & T. Clark, 1988).

16. 'Battered into Submission', in *Christianity Today* volume 33, June 16 1989, 26. In their book *Battered into Submission* (Downers Grove: InterVarsity, 1989), the Alsdurfs argue that (in the US) violence is actually more prevalent in Christian homes than it is in the population at large. The detailed research does not exist to make the same claim for Britain, but our field work uncovered a very substantial problem for the British churches here.

6. *The Family and the Church*

1. The Uniting Church in Australia has set an example that others could do well to follow, with a clearly-defined official policy on the role of the church in supporting family life. See the various documents in the series of *Children and Your Church Strategy Papers*, including especially *Developing a Family Focus, Involving Children in Worship, Social Issues Affecting Children* (all Melbourne: Uniting Church Press, 1989).

2. On the question of all-age or intergenerational worship, see David Ng & Virginia Thomas, *Children in the Worshiping Community* (Atlanta: John Knox Press, 1981); Megan Coote, *Growing Together* (Melbourne: JBCE, 1988); Peter Graystone & Eileen Turner, *A Church for All Ages* (London: Scripture Union, 1993). For a helpful series of case studies, see David Merritt & Muriel Porter, *What will we do with the Children?* (Melbourne: JBCE, 1990).

3. Cf. Rodney Clapp, *Families at the Crossroads*, 114-32.

4. For one of the most useful explorations of this theme, see John H. Westerhoff III, *Living the Faith Community* (San Francisco: Harper & Row, 1985); also (from a different angle) Rosemary Radford Ruether, 'Church & Family', in *New Blackfriars* 65 (1984), 202-12.

5. John Drane, *Evangelism for a New Age*, 115-48.

6. Raymond Fung, 'Mission in Christ's Way', in *International Review of Mission* LXXIX (1990), 82-103.

7. See Robert & Julia Banks, *The Church Comes Home* (Sutherland NSW: Albatross, 1986); Robert Banks, *Going to Church in the First Century* (Parramatta NSW: Hexagon, 1985).

7. *Supporting Parents and Children*

1. Margaret Hebblethwaite, *Motherhood and God* (London: Geoffrey Chapman, 1984); John Finney, *Finding Faith Today* (Swindon: Bible Society, 1992), 40-1. His research shows that the family in general is a significant influence in the lives of people coming to faith in Christ.

2. John Finney, *op. cit.*, 41.
3. Cf. John Drane, *Evangelism for a New Age*; Raymond Fung, *The Isaiah Vision* (Geneva: World Council of Churches, 1992).
4. On storytelling, see Janet Litherland, *Storytelling from the Bible* (Colorado Springs: Meriwether, 1991); Thomas E. Boomershine, *Story Journey* (Nashville: Abingdon Press, 1988); and for a theological angle, Terrence W. Tilley, *Story Theology* (Collegeville MN: Liturgical Press, 1990).
5. John Naisbitt & Patricia Aburdene, *Megatrends 2000* (London: Pan, 1990), 53-76.
6. For more on dance, cf. Martin Blogg, *Healing in the Dance* (Eastbourne: Kingsway, 1988); Valerie Preston-Dunlop, *A Handbook for Dance Education* (London: Longman, 1980). And for specific ideas, see Ronald Gagne, Thomas Kane & Robert VerEecke, *Introducing Dance in Christian Worship* (Washington DC: Pastoral Press, 1984); Carla De Sola, *The Spirit Moves* (Austin TX: The Sharing Company, 1977); Constance Fisher, *Dancing with Early Christians* (Austin TX: The Sharing Company, 1983); Dane Packard, *The Church Becoming Christ's Body* (Austin TX: The Sharing Company, 1985); Doug Adams, *Dancing Christmas Carols* (San Jose CA: Resource Publications, 1978). But remember that dance cannot be learned from books, and needs to reflect local culture.
7. On mask-making, see further John Drane, *Evangelism for a New Age*, 40-1; and Doug Adams, 'Facing the Cain in Ourselves', in *Church Teachers* 20/2 (1992), 58-9.
8. On this see, for example, James Fowler, *Becoming Adult, Becoming Christian* (San Francisco: Harper & Row, 1984); Janet Hagberg & Robert A. Guelich, *The Critical Journey* (Dallas: Word, 1989).
9. John H. Westerhoff III, *Will Our Children Have Faith?* (San Francisco: Harper & Row, 1976); see also his *Bringing Up Children in the Christian Faith* (Minneapolis: Winston Press, 1980). For a popular presentation of this thinking from a British perspective, see the report of the Church of England General Synod Board of Education, *How Faith Grows* (London: Church House Publishing,

1991). On how this view correlates with the scriptural evidence, see John Drane, *Evangelism for a New Age*, 87-114.

10. For an informative, if occasionally intemperate, analysis of the issues involved, see Norman Dennis & George Erdos, *Families Without Fatherhood* (London: IEA Health & Welfare Unit, 1993).

11. For an extended account of the American experience, see Joseph P. Shapiro & Joannie M. Schrof, 'Honor Thy Children', in *US News* 118/8 (February 27 1995), 39-49.

12. Kathryn Goering Reid with Marie M. Fortune, *Preventing Child Sexual Abuse: A Curriculum for Children Ages 9 through 12* (New York: United Church Press, 1989).

8. From Teenage to Third Age

1. Australian churches have generally taken work with families much more seriously than those in the UK. As well as its policy for Children and the Church, the Uniting Church in Australia has also led the way in developing an official policy for young people. See *Young People and Your Church* (Melbourne: Uniting Church Press 1989), produced in two parts, as *A Policy for Action* and *Action Manual*.

2. For a succinct historical and theological account of the issues involved, see L. William Countryman, *Dirt, Greed and Sex* (Philadelphia: Fortress Press, 1988).

3. The whole question of homosexuality is of course a highly controversial matter in some sections of the Church. The main issues and history of the debate are well documented in Peter Coleman, *Gay Christians* (London: SCM, 1989). From a practical pastoral point of view, gay and lesbian teenagers (and adults) are no different than others: they need love, support, acceptance and understanding.

4. To do this in a useful way, we would need to equip our teenagers to know how to share the responsibilities of parenthood equally, rather than beginning from stereotyped patriarchal concepts. Leaders interested in exploring this will find some interesting ideas in Carrie Carmichael, *Non-Sexist Childraising* (Boston:

Beacon, 1977); and Selma Greenberg, *Right from the Start* (Boston: Houghton Mifflin, 1978), though materials that could actually be used in a group are less easy to come by.

5. See Timothy H. Brubaker, *Family Relationships in Later Life* (New York: Sage, 1990 2nd ed).

6. Westerhoff, *Living the Faith Community*, 9-10.

9. Ministering to Families in Crisis

1. For an example of this approach in action, see John Drane, *Evangelism for a New Age*, 165-73.

2. Erin Pizzey, *Scream Quietly or the Neighbours Will Hear* (London: Penguin, 1974).

3. The connexion from the one to the other has been a recurring theme throughout history, and ultimately goes back to the Greek dualism between body and spirit, and the (male) belief that men represent the spirit, women the flesh. Since on this understanding, salvation could only come through escape from the flesh into the spirit, we are not surprised to find women have suffered as a result at all periods of history. Roger de Caen wrote in 1095 that 'If [a woman's] bowels and flesh were cut open, you would see what filth is covered by her white skin . . . There is no plague which monks should dread more than a woman . . .' Luther wrote that 'A woman is not fully the master of herself', and also recommended she should be 'like a nail driven into the wall' (by her husband). Calvin accepted the right of a man to beat his wife, and specifically stated that such beating was not a reason for her to leave him, unless her life was in danger: 'She must not deviate from the duty which she has before God to please her husband, but be faithful whatever happens.' For more extensive discussion of these attitudes and their philosophical background, see Joy M. K. Bussert, *Battered Women*, 5-15, 55-66; Rita-Lou Clarke, *Pastoral Care of Battered Women* (Philadelphia: Westminster Press, 1986), 321-35.

4. 'Battered into Submission', in *Christianity Today* vol. 33 (June 16 1989), 24.

5. Quoted in Bussert, *Battered Women*, 61.

6. Cf. Randy Christian, 'Three Strategies to Prevent Abuse', in *Leadership* 11 (spring 1990), 96-101.

7. Marie M. Fortune, *Keeping the Faith* (San Francisco; Harper San Francisco, 1987).

8. Clarke, *Pastoral Care of Battered Women*, 87. For invaluable practical guidance, see the whole of chapter 4 in this book, 86-110.

9. Cf. Gary P. Liaboe, 'The Place of Wife Battering in Considering Divorce', in *Journal of Psychology and Theology* 13 (1985), 129-38.

10. For the cycle, see Lenore Walker, *The Battered Woman* (New York: Harper & Row, 1979; also R. E. & R. P. Dobash, *Violence Against Wives*.

11. The expression of Richard Gelles, *The Violent Home* (Beverly Hills CA: Sage 1972), 74.

12. For this reason, helping men who are also religious to overcome their violent tendencies can be a particularly tough assignment: see A. L. Horton & J. A. Williamson (eds), *Abuse and Religion: When Praying Isn't Enough* (Lexington MA: Lexington University Press, 1988).

13. Bussert, *Battered Women*, 45 (her italics).

14. For a general account of the psychological dimensions of what may be going on in violent relationships, see Rita-Lou Clarke, *Pastoral Care of Battered Women*, 36-60.

15. Cf. Marie M. Fortune, 'The Nature of Abuse', in *Pastoral Psychology* 41/5 (1993), 275-88.

16. Cf. Blair & Rita Justice, *The Abusing Family* (New York: Human Sciences Press 1976).

17. Cf. Michael J. Garanzini, 'Troubled Homes: Pastoral Responses to Violent and Abusive Families', in *Pastoral Psychology* 36/4 (1988), 218-29.

18. Clyde Narramore, 'Abusing Children Emotionally', in *Fundamentalist Journal* 5/5 (1986), 32-4. This conclusion is all the more remarkable in view of the fact that this author elsewhere advocates a hierarchical view of the family.

19. For more on handling abuse stemming from religious faith, see Wesley R. Monfalcone, *Coping With Abuse in the Family*

(Philadelphia: Westminster Press 1980), 45-57.

20. For more on the pastoral implications of sexual abuse, see Mary D. Pellauer, Barbara Chester & Jane A. Boyaiian (eds), *Sexual Assault and Abuse: A Handbook for Clergy and Religious Professionals*; *Child Abuse* (Edinburgh: Church of Scotland Board of Social Responsibility, 1990); Anne Peake & Khadj Rouf, *Working with Sexually Abused Children* (London: Children's Society, 1991); Hilary Cashman, *Christianity and Child Sexual Abuse* (London: SPCK, 1993).

21. For a suitable training programme, see Marie M. Fortune, *Violence in the Family. A Workshop Curriculum for Clergy and Other Helpers* (Cleveland OH: Pilgrim Press 1991.

22. For documentation of this, see Florence Rush, *The Best Kept Secret: Sexual Abuse of Children* (New York: McGraw-Hill, 1980), 80-122.

23. Cf. Florence Rush, *The Best Kept Secret*, 170-82.

24. Randy Frame, 'Child Abuse: The Church's Best Kept Secret?', in *Christianity Today* 29/3 (Feb 15 1985), 34. For helpful insights on the theological significance of abuse, see James N. Poling, 'Child Sexual Abuse: A Rich Context for Thinking about God, Community, and Ministry', in *Journal of Pastoral Care* XLII/1 (1988), 58-61. On the broader religious ramifications, cf. Ann Loades, *Thinking about Child Sexual Abuse* (London: University of London, 1994); Joanne Carlson Brown & Carole R. Bohn (eds), *Christianity, Patriarchy and Abuse* (Cleveland OH: Pilgrim Press, 1989).

25. Jennifer Craven, 'Sexual Abuse in Children: Factors, Effects, Treatment, and Ministry Implications', in *Christian Education Journal* 7/1 (1986), 73. For a case study of effective ways to help parents of abused children, see Frances Rickford, 'You Must Have Known', in *Social Work Today* 23/19 (January 23, 1992), 14-15.

26. See Marie M. Fortune, *Sexual Violence: the Unmentionable Sin* (New York: Pilgrim Press, 1983), 176-89. For more on work with perpetrators, cf. Graham C. Willis, *Unspeakable Crimes* (London: Children's Society 1993), which is especially useful as it documents and compares the British and North American experience.

27. But this is not the only cause: cf. Alfred Kadushin & Judith A. Martin, *Child Abuse: An Interactional Event* (New York: Columbia University Press, 1981), who identify the key components of abuse as being within the abusive event itself.

BOOKLIST

Elizabeth Achtemeier, *Preaching about Family Relationships* (Philadelphia: Westminster Press, 1987).

Bert N. Adams, *The Family: a Sociological Interpretation* (Chicago: Rand McNally, 1975).

Graham Allan, *Family Life* (Oxford: Blackwell, 1985).

James & Phyllis Alsdurf, *Battered into Submission* (Downers Grove: InterVarsity, 1989).

Ruth Nanda Anshen, *The Family: its Function and Destiny* (New York: Harper & Row, 1959).

Jack O. Balswick & Judith K. Balswick, *The Family* (Grand Rapids: Baker, 1991).

Jack O.Balswick, *Men at the Crossroads* (Downers Grove: InterVarsity, 1992).

Stephen Barton, 'Marriage & Family Life as Christian Concerns', in *The Expository Times* 106/3 (1994), 69-74.

N. W. Bell & E. F. Vogel, *A Modern Introduction to the Family* (New York: Free Press, 1968).

Brigitte Berger & Peter L. Berger, *The War Over the Family* (London: Hutchinson, 1983).

P. G. Boss, W. J. Doherty, R. LaRossa, W. R. Schumm & S. K. Steinmetz (eds), *Sourcebook of Family Theories & Methods* (New York: Plenum Press, 1993).

S. Brody & S. Axelrod, *Mothers, Fathers & Children* (New York: International University Press, 1978).

Joanne Carlson Brown & Carole R. Bohn (eds), *Christianity, Patriarchy and Abuse* (Cleveland OH: Pilgrim Press, 1989).

Timothy H. Brubaker, *Family Relationships in Later Life* (New York: Sage, 1990 2nd ed.).

Joy M. K. Bussert, *Battered Women. From a Theology of Suffering to an Ethic of Empowerment* (Minneapolis: Division for Mission of the Lutheran Church in America, 1986).

Carrie Carmichael, *Non-Sexist Childraising* (Boston: Beacon, 1977).

Gwen B. Carr, *Marriage and Family in a Decade of Change* (Reading MA: Addison Wesley, 1977).

James Casey, *The History of the Family* (Oxford: Blackwell, 1989).

Rodney Clapp, *Families at the Crossroads* (Downers Grove: InterVarsity, 1993).

Randy Christian, 'Three Strategies to Prevent Abuse', in *Leadership* 11 (spring 1990), 96-101.

Rita-Lou Clarke, *Pastoral Care of Battered Women* (Philadelphia: Westminster Press, 1986).

Robert Coles, *The Spiritual Life of Children* (London: HarperCollins, 1992).

Pamela Cooper-White, 'Soul Stealing: Power Relations in Pastoral Sexual Abuse', in *The Christian Century* 108 (February 20 1991), 196-9.

Megan Coote, *Growing Together* (Melbourne: JBCE, 1988).

L. William Countryman, *Dirt, Greed and Sex* (Philadelphia: Fortress Press, 1988).

Jennifer Craven, 'Sexual Abuse in Children: Factors, Effects, Treatment, and Ministry Implications', in *Christian Education Journal* 7/1 (1986), 69-78.

Jon Davies (ed), *The Family: Is It Just Another Lifestyle Choice?* (London: IEA Health & Welfare Unit, 1993).

Norman Dennis & George Erdos, *Families Without Fatherhood* (London: IEA Health & Welfare Unit, 1993).

R. Emerson Dobash & Russell Dobash, *Violence Against Wives: A Case against the Patriarchy* (New York: The Free Press, 1979).

Mary Farmer, *The Family* (London: Longman, 1970).

Marie M. Fortune, *Sexual Violence: the Unmentionable Sin* (New York:

Pilgrim Press, 1983).

Marie M. Fortune, *Keeping the Faith: Questions and Answers for the Abused Woman* (San Francisco: HarperSanFrancisco, 1987).

Marie M. Fortune, *Violence in the Family. A Workshop Curriculum for Clergy and Other Helpers* (Cleveland OH: Pilgrim Press, 1991).

Marie M. Fortune, 'The Nature of Abuse', in *Pastoral Psychology* 41/5 (1993), 275-88.

James Fowler, *Becoming Adult, Becoming Christian* (San Francisco: Harper & Row, 1984).

Randy Frame, 'Child Abuse: The Church's Best Kept Secret?', in *Christianity Today* 29/3 (Feb 15 1985), 32-4.

Leslie J. Francis, *Making Contact: Christian Nurture, Family Worship & Church Growth* (London: Collins, 1986).

Frank F. Furstenberg & Graham B. Spanier, *Recycling the Family: Remarriage after Divorce* (Beverly Hills CA: Sage, 1984).

Kathleen M. Galvin & Bernard J. Brommel, *Family Communication* (New York: HarperCollins, 1991).

Michael J. Garanzini, 'Troubled Homes: Pastoral Responses to Violent and Abusive Families', in *Pastoral Psychology* 36/4 (1988), 218-29.

Richard Gelles, *The Violent Home* (Beverly Hills CA: Sage, 1972).

Diana Gittins, *The Family in Question* (London: Macmillan, 1993 2nd ed.).

David Goetz, 'Is the Pastor's Family Safe at Home?', in *Leadership* 13/4 (1992), 38-44.

Willystine Goodsell, *A History of Marriage and the Family* (New York: Macmillan, 1934).

A. E. Gottfried & A. W. Gottfried, *Redefining Families* (New York: Plenum, 1994).

B. Gottlieb, *The Family in the Western World* (New York: OUP, 1993).

Peter Graystone & Eileen Turner, *A Church for All Ages* (London: Scripture Union, 1993).

Selma Greenberg, *Right from the Start* (Boston: Houghton Mifflin, 1978).

Janet Hagberg & Robert A. Guelich, *The Critical Journey* (Dallas: Word, 1989).

C. C. Harris, *The Family: an Introduction* (London: Allen & Unwin, 1969).

Margaret Hebblethwaite, *Motherhood and God* (London: Geoffrey Chapman, 1984).

A. L. Horton & J. A. Williamson (eds), *Abuse and Religion: When Praying Isn't Enough* (Lexington MA: Lexington University Press, 1988).

Blair & Rita Justice, *The Abusing Family* (New York: Human Sciences Press, 1976).

Jill Krementz, *How it Feels when Parents Divorce* (London: Victor Gollancz, 1985).

Andrew D. Lester (ed), *When Children Suffer: A Sourcebook for Ministry with Children in Crisis* (Philadelphia: Westminster Press, 1987).

Ann Loades, *Thinking about Child Sexual Abuse* (London: University of London, 1994).

Brenda Maddox, *The Half-Parent: Living with Other People's Children* (London: Andre Deutsch, 1975).

Marianne Maley, 'The Christian Family', in *Coracle* 3/2 (1989), 5-6.

G. L. Martin, *Counseling for Family Violence and Abuse* (Waco: Word, 1987).

David Merritt & Muriel Porter, *What will we do with the Children?* (Melbourne: JBCE, 1990).

Al Miles, 'Healing Scars of Childhood Abuse', in *Leadership* 13/3 (1992), 58-63.

Errol Miller, *Men at Risk* (Kingston: Jamaica Publishing House, 1991).

Mintel, *Family Lifestyles* (London: Mintel, 1993).

Wesley R. Monfalcone, *Coping with Abuse in the Family* (Philadelphia: Westminster Press, 1980).

Patricia Morgan, *Farewell to the Family? Public Policy and Family Breakdown in Britain and the USA* (London: Institute of Economic Affairs, 1995).

Clyde Narramore, 'Abusing Children Emotionally', in *Fundamentalist Journal* 5/5 (1986), 32-4.

James Nelson, *The Intimate Connection: Male Sexuality, Masculine Spirituality* (Philadelphia: Westminster Press, 1988).

David Ng & Virginia Thomas, *Children in the Worshiping Community*

(Atlanta: John Knox Press, 1981).

Alan Nichols, Joan Clarke & Trevor Hogan, *Transforming Families and Communities* (Sydney: AIO Press, 1987).

Anne Peake & Khadj Rouf, *Working with Sexually Abused Children* (London: Children's Society, 1991).

Mary D. Pellauer, Barbara Chester & Jane A. Boyaiian (eds), *Sexual Assault and Abuse: A Handbook for Clergy and Religious Professionals* (San Francisco: Harper & Row, 1987).

Erin Pizzey, *Scream Quietly or the Neighbours Will Hear* (London: Penguin, 1974).

James N. Poling, 'Child Sexual Abuse: A Rich Context for Thinking about God, Community, and Ministry', in *Journal of Pastoral Care* XLII/1 (1988), 58-61.

R. N. Rapoport, M. P. Fogarty & R. Rapoport (eds), *Families in Britain* (London: Routledge & Kegan Paul, 1982).

Kathryn Goering Reid with Marie M. Fortune, *Preventing Child Sexual Abuse: A Curriculum for Children Ages 9 through 12* (New York: United Church Press, 1989).

Rosemary Radford Ruether, 'Church & Family', in *New Blackfriars* 65 (1984), 202-12.

Florence Rush, *The Best Kept Secret: Sexual Abuse of Children* (New York: McGraw-Hill, 1980).

Lindell Sawyers (ed), *Faith and Families* (Philadelphia: Geneva Press, 1986).

A. C. Robin Skynner, *One Flesh: Separate Persons* (London: Constable, 1976).

Robin Skynner & John Cleese, *Families and How to Survive Them* (London: Methuen, 1983).

Kay Marshall Strom, *Helping Women in Crisis* (Grand Rapids: Zondervan, 1986).

Judson J. Swihart & Steven L. Brigham, *Helping Children of Divorce* (London: Scripture Union, 1982).

Barrie Thorne & Marilyn Yaloms (eds), *Rethinking the Family* (London: Longman, 1982).

Yvette Walczak, *Divorce: the Child's Point of View* (London: Harper & Row, 1984).

Lenore Walker, *The Battered Woman* (New York: Harper & Row, 1979).

Laura Sherman Walters, *There's a New Family in My House. Blending Stepfamilies Together* (Wheaton IL: Harold Shaw Publishers, 1993).

John H. Westerhoff III, *Will Our Children Have Faith?* (San Francisco: Harper & Row, 1976).

John H. Westerhoff III, *Bringing Up Children in the Christian Faith* (Minneapolis: Winston Press, 1980).

John H. Westerhoff III, *Living the Faith Community* (San Francisco: Harper & Row, 1985).

David Will & Robert M. Wrate, *Integrated Family Therapy* (London: Tavistock, 1985).

Graham C. Willis, *Unspeakable Crimes* (London: Children's Society, 1993).

Adrian Wilson, *Family* (London: Tavistock, 1985).

Robert F. Winch, *The Modern Family* (New York: Rinehart & Winston, 1971).

INDEX

120077